GW00992124

seeing**red** 2015

The 2015 MCE Insurance British Superbike Championship was one that featured arguably two of the fiercest rivals in recent years going head to head for the title; Britain versus Australia is one of the oldest rivalries in sport and Josh Brookes v Shane Byrne was no different.

It is renowned that the rivalry between the pair since the 2014 season is steely – if they are together then you could cut the atmosphere with a knife and there is certainly not a lot of love between them, but that became one of the storylines of the 2015 season.

Josh has been in a good place this season and was on fire for much of it with the new Yamaha YZF-R1 and after much pre-season anticipation it lived up to expectation and after the early development showed he was going to be the rider to beat. Josh has been runner-up twice before, third placed once and fourth placed twice and he certainly didn't want to miss out again.

There was certainly a point in the mid-season when we thought perhaps the pendulum had well and truly swung in Shakey's direction and then as it turned out it went very firmly the other way, which was unknown territory for the defending champion, but he did try and claw his way back right until the end.

2015 again delivered some dramatic races across the twelve rounds and 26 races. The championship continues to surpass its rivals because of the hard work and dedication of the teams and riders in the series who strive for success each season and recognition has to go to them for their achievements.

This season we have had lap records obliterated and new riders making their mark on the championship which proves that the support classes in Britain can really be the stepping stone to bigger things. I was particularly impressed with rookies Luke Mossey and Danny Buchan, the pair stepping up from the Supersport and Superstock classes respectively – scoring podium finishes in their debut season with Mossey also lifting the Rider's Cup honours ahead of many of his more experienced competitors.

I feel one of the highlights of this season has been how many teams and riders have celebrated podium success – we have had six different race winners, but in addition to those, an incredible nine further riders have appeared on the podium this year. Eleven different teams appeared on the podium over the 26 races representing five different manufacturers showing how the existing technical regulations deliver a level playing field.

A special mention has to go to Tyco BMW for their first win with the new manufacturer, Smiths Racing for Billy McConnell claiming their first podium at Cadwell Park after moving into MCE BSB and finally Lloyds British Moto Rapido Ducati who celebrated their first podium with John Hopkins at the season finale – the first time for the Ducati Panigale in the championship.

The decider for the top six was the closest it has ever been since the Showdown was introduced, but in the end it again impressively featured five different teams and four manufacturers, which makes me extremely proud of MCE BSB and already we have some exciting changes for next year including Shakey's return to Ducati with the Be Wiser PBM team, 2011 champion Tommy Hill's new ePayMe Yamaha team with former rival John Hopkins and Stuart Easton, plus James Ellison already confirmed for another season with GBmoto.

In the support classes the Motorpoint British Supersport Championship characteristically produced a brilliant season with the Profile Racing team winning the title for the first time with Luke Stapleford. Five different race winners and a further three different podium finishers made it another hallmark season of Supersport racing.

As always I would like to extend our thanks to all of our championship partners, teams and riders across the classes and to my organising colleagues who continue to make MCE BSB grow in strength and stature throughout the world. Finally, a thank you to the media who write and capture the drama and passion of a year in MCE BSB, and of course to the fans whose enthusiasm and devotion to following the series every round is tremendous.

Congratulations to 2015 champion Josh Brookes. I hope you enjoy the season in images from Double Red and we hope that this leaves you wanting even more as we begin the countdown to the 2016 season.

Stuart Higgs
Series Director
MCE Insurance British Superbike Championship

Published in 2015 by
The Original Double Red Ltd
4 Gateway Court
Dankerwood Road
South Hykeham
Lincoln LN6 9UL
Tel: +44 (0)1522 693 278
www.doublered.co.uk

ISBN 978-0-9927465-2-0

Photography: Copyright and all other rights to the images
and content of this book remain the property of
The Original Double Red Ltd

Photographers
James Wright
Keith Lock
Sue Ward
Dave Yeomans
Peter Denton
Bonnie Lane (Ducati TriOptions Cup)

Project Manager
Sue Ward

Picture Editors
James Wright
Sue Ward
Katie Ward

Contributing Editor
Larry Carter

Contributors
Dave Fern
Sue Carter
Phil Wain

Design and Layout
Kubed Design

Results and Statistics
Timing Solutions Ltd. www.tsl-timing.com

Special Thanks to:
The organisers and sponsors involved in the MCE Insurance British Superbike Championship, especially the team at MSVR whose dedication and commitment makes the MCE Insurance British Superbike Championship the strongest domestic championship in the world. Every single person involved in the organisation and running of the championship whose often difficult jobs go unnoticed and unrewarded - they know who they are: the medics, physios, marshals, press officers, scrutineers, journalists, television crews, truck drivers, mechanics, chefs, cleaners, hospitality crews, commentators etc, and last but not least the riders and teams, who seldom complain at 'just one more shot' and who make the MCE Insurance British Superbike Championship the amazing spectacle it is.

Contents

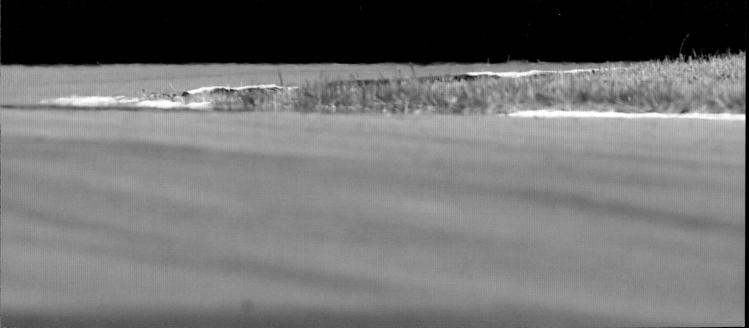

It's moments like this words aren't enough. It's a feeling to win a championship and that I can't say in simple words.

The big public moment is stood on the podium . . . still in your leathers, adrenalin in your blood, smelling of champagne, being handed the trophy and the crowd cheering on your success.

The real and less climactic moment is some time later, it's not a specific moment but a process of reflection. Going through all the years in your head, thinking of all the hard times and having an equal or better good memory to balance it, but it will never balance up without a championship.

From 14 years ago since I started racing on tarmac, half of it has been in BSB. Seven hard years of bashing bars in the British Championship can only be justified by winning. Returning each year to right the wrongs, push harder and find more, because it will have all been for nothing if you don't lift the cup. If getting pole positions and setting lap records throughout the season wasn't enough, it was the twice 'triple double' that was my highlight of 2015.

I've not done it alone. Thanks to Shaun Muir and Dale McElveen at Milwaukee, the SMR team have gone to the top level, without a doubt the best team in the championship. Every person in the team, in their own way has contributed to my success.

Stewart Winton and Ian Lord have made this dream a reality. What they have done with the bike and also with me, has been clear to see.

Thank you to all the sponsors, some of which have now become great friends, financial support is critical and my safety products have been first class. And thanks to everyone for supporting me, from fans to family . . . you're all great!

The most important 'thank you' is to my partner Aimie, she is beside me always and makes me who I am . . .

Josh Brookes #25
MCE British Superbike Champion 2015

Josh Brookes
Milwaukee Yamaha

After six years of trying whereby he fell short of the title by varying margins, 2015 proved seventh heaven for Josh Brookes as he ended up taking the crown in relatively easy fashion in all honesty. It really was a season of two halves for the oft-controversial Aussie as both he and the Milwaukee Yamaha team learned the traits of the brand-new R1 for the first few rounds, racking up the podiums but, amazingly, not managing a victory until the halfway point of the season. But from Brands Hatch onwards, it was a tale of supremacy whereby Brookes and the Yamaha proved a virtually unbeatable combination as they dominated the second half of the season. At the same time, the challenge from arch-rival Byrne faltered and it all meant that Brookes lifted the title with two races to spare. His only blip of the whole season was a crash in the very last race of the season proving even champions make occasional mistakes, but by then, the championship-winning party had already started.

Results			
Position:			1st
Points:			703
Qualifying Poles:			6
Fastest Lap Poles:			6
Front Rows:			7
Best Grid:			Pole
Races:			26
Wins:			13
Podiums:			10
Best Result:			1st
Fastest Laps:			11
Donington Park:	3rd	6th	
Brands Hatch Indy:	3rd	3rd	
Oulton Park:	2nd	3rd	
Snetterton:	2nd	2nd	
Knockhill:	3rd	3rd	
Brands Hatch GP:	1st	1st	
Thruxton:	1st	1st	
Cadwell Park:	1st	1st	
Oulton Park:	4th	1st	2nd
TT Circuit Assen:	1st	1st	
Silverstone:	1st	1st	
Brands Hatch GP:	1st	1st	C

Shane Byrne
PBM Be Wiser Kawasaki

In most other seasons, Shane Byrne would have been British Champion having won seven races and with a points tally just shy of what he won his fourth MCE BSB crown with just twelve months previous. Despite a broken hand in pre-season testing, the first half of the season looked to be going great for Shakey as he dominated the early season races, but the first of three significant factors, which were ultimately to see his downfall, happened when Ryuichi Kiyonari took him down at Oulton Park. A big crash at Brands Hatch affected his performance for a couple of rounds, but the third significant factor was a mechanical failure on the second visit to Oulton Park which robbed him of another potential win. He gamely gave chase to the dominant Brookes but with no wins in the all-important Showdown, to Brookes' six, meant Byrne and his PBM team will be back to try to claim title number five next season, this time with factory Ducati power at their disposal.

Results			
Position:			2nd
Points:			662
Qualifying Poles:			4
Fastest Lap Poles:			5
Front Rows:			6
Best Grid:			Pole
Races:			26
Wins:			7
Podiums:			10
Best Result:			1st
Fastest Laps:			9
Donington Park:	2nd	1st	
Brands Hatch Indy:	2nd	2nd	
Oulton Park:	3rd	C	
Snetterton:	1st	1st	
Knockhill:	1st	1st	
Brands Hatch GP:	C	2nd	
Thruxton:	4th	2nd	
Cadwell Park:	6th	4th	
Oulton Park:	1st	R	1st
TT Circuit Assen:	4th	5th	
Silverstone:	2nd	5th	
Brands Hatch GP:	2nd	2nd	3rd

James Ellison
JG Speedfit Kawasaki

So often dubbed one of the unluckiest riders in the series, whereby injury has blighted his recent attempts to land the British crown, 2015 represented James Ellison's best shot at it in recent times as with a competitive JG Speedfit Kawasaki at his disposal once again, he started the season as one of the favourites. That early season promise was justified as the Cumbrian took three wins in the opening four races, but that momentum couldn't be maintained as the season rolled on. In typical Ellison fashion, things took a turn for the worse when he crashed during a sudden rain shower during qualifying at Snetterton, breaking ribs in the process. Then at Thruxton, he went down on someone else's oil and broke his wrist which ruled him out again. He bounced back to secure his place in the Showdown and a double podium behind Brookes at Assen showed promise, but a duff tyre at Silverstone saw him score no points in race two and his challenge was effectively over.

Results			
Position:			3rd
Points:			614
Qualifying Poles:			1
Fastest Lap Poles:			2
Front Rows:			6
Best Grid:			Pole
Races:			23
Wins:			3
Podiums:			6
Best Result:			1st
Fastest Laps:			4
Donington Park:	1st	12th	
Brands Hatch Indy:	1st	1st	
Oulton Park:	6th	2nd	
Snetterton:	R	7th	
Knockhill:	C	R	
Brands Hatch GP:	3rd	4th	
Thruxton:	C	Inj	
Cadwell Park:	Inj	Inj	
Oulton Park:	2nd	5th	5th
TT Circuit Assen:	2nd	2nd	
Silverstone:	5th	17th	
Brands Hatch GP:	6th	5th	2nd

Michael Laverty
Tyco BMW Motorrad

It's fair to say that Michael Laverty's season was very slow to start, but ended in fantastic fashion as he got stronger as the year progressed. Back from MotoGP duty, it took the Ulsterman a while to adapt to the production-based rules of MCE BSB which wasn't helped by his contract to still test the Bridgestone tyres in MotoGP. However, despite his lack of podiums in the greater part of the season, Laverty steadily racked up the points and was unlucky not to climb the podium at Knockhill when he was penalised for a yellow flag infringement. A couple of minor blips apart, Michael got stronger and after qualifying for the Showdown, we got to see what he could really do aboard the 2015 BMW. Three podiums and a win propelled him to fourth in the standings in the final three races, meaning the end of the season came all too quickly for him and if he remains with the team as expected, he's sure to be a major contender in 2016.

Results			
Position:			4th
Points:			601
Qualifying Poles:			0
Fastest Lap Poles:			0
Front Rows:			2
Best Grid:			P2
Races:			26
Wins:			1
Podiums:			3
Best Result:			1st
Fastest Laps:			0
Donington Park:	9th	7th	
Brands Hatch Indy:	13th	19th	
Oulton Park:	8th	4th	
Snetterton:	R	4th	
Knockhill:	4th	6th	
Brands Hatch GP:	5th	5th	
Thruxton:	9th	6th	
Cadwell Park:	5th	C	
Oulton Park:	9th	7th	12th
TT Circuit Assen:	3rd	9th	
Silverstone:	6th	2nd	
Brands Hatch GP:	9th	3rd	1st

Dan Linfoot
Honda Racing

Fifth again for the likeable Yorkshireman in what proved to be a challenging season at times. It all started off so well at Donington Park when he ran Shane Byrne close for the victory and laid his cards firmly on the table as a major championship contender this season. But then came free practice at Brands Hatch two weeks later and a nasty crash saw him sustain a badly broken wrist which saw him miss four vital races. He came back at Snetterton but what followed set the scene for the remainder of the season. Lacklustre free practice and sometimes qualifying sessions saw him struggling down the order, meaning a huge effort was needed on race day which sometimes he managed and sometimes he didn't. The fact he got in the Showdown in such a competitive season says something about Linfoot and his ability, as highlighted by his podiums at Thruxton, Oulton Park and Silverstone, but the tyre gamble at Assen apart, it was probably a little disappointing by his high standards.

Results

Position:	5th		
Points:	556		
Qualifying Poles:	0		
Fastest Lap Poles:	1		
Front Rows:	2		
Best Grid:	Pole		
Races:	22		
Wins:	0		
Podiums:	4		
Best Result:	2nd		
Fastest Laps:	1		
Donington Park:	4th	2nd	
Brands Hatch Indy:	Inj	Inj	
Oulton Park:	Inj	Inj	
Snetterton:	5th	10th	
Knockhill:	C	12th	
Brands Hatch GP:	8th	C	
Thruxton:	2nd	5th	
Cadwell Park:	10th	10th	
Oulton Park:	5th	3rd	6th
TT Circuit Assen:	14th	22nd	
Silverstone:	7th	3rd	
Brands Hatch GP:	13th	10th	4th

Tommy Bridewell
Tyco BMW Motorrad

When things are going right for Tommy Bridewell, he is one of the fastest and most naturally talented riders in the paddock, but when things are not 100%, he becomes a different animal and if any season exposed that, it was 2015. A new team for the rider who finished third in last year's title race and a new bike to boot, but in truth, he never really got going. A brilliant victory in the opening race at Oulton Park was followed by a crash in race two and that kind of epitomised Bridewell's season, and maybe his career to date. Changes to the bike affected his confidence, but he always gave it his all and sometimes that meant he over-rode it with the resulting consequences which saw seven DNFs because of crashes. His terrier-like persona wouldn't let him stop challenging and although he may have been fighting a losing battle this season, a change of bike and team will herald a stronger challenge for 2016 honours one would expect.

Results

Position:	6th		
Points:	545		
Qualifying Poles:	0		
Fastest Lap Poles:	0		
Front Rows:	3		
Best Grid:	P2		
Races:	26		
Wins:	1		
Podiums:	2		
Best Result:	1st		
Fastest Laps:	0		
Donington Park:	6th	8th	
Brands Hatch Indy:	C	6th	
Oulton Park:	1st	C	
Snetterton:	4th	5th	
Knockhill:	7th	C	
Brands Hatch GP:	4th	C	
Thruxton:	C	4th	
Cadwell Park:	4th	3rd	
Oulton Park:	R	C	3rd
TT Circuit Assen:	8th	C	
Silverstone:	9th	7th	
Brands Hatch GP:	11th	11th	12th

Luke Mossey
Quattro Plant Tec-care Kawasaki

Squeezing into the points in the opening races of your rookie season is a fantastic achievement in itself in the toughest domestic race series of its kind on the planet and that's exactly what Luke Mossey did from the off. But the natural progression is then to start finishing in the top ten and it wasn't long before the Cambridgeshire youngster was doing that in what was turning out to be a textbook season on what was very modest machinery. Therefore, no one should have been surprised when Mossey started running up with the established stars from mid season and when he scored a podium at Thruxton, it really was just reward for his and the team's efforts. But that was just the beginning and from then on, he was regularly challenging, scoring another podium in tricky conditions at Assen after leading the race. Not many people would have had him down to win the MCE Rider's Cup at the start of the year, but that's exactly what he did and he thoroughly deserved it.

Results

Position:	7th		
Points:	168		
Qualifying Poles:	0		
Fastest Lap Poles:	0		
Front Rows:	2		
Best Grid:	P2		
Races:	26		
Wins:	0		
Podiums:	2		
Best Result:	3rd		
Fastest Laps:	0		
Donington Park:	15th	19th	
Brands Hatch Indy:	12th	24th	
Oulton Park:	R	13th	
Snetterton:	9th	13th	
Knockhill:	8th	C	
Brands Hatch GP:	7th	7th	
Thruxton:	6th	3rd	
Cadwell Park:	7th	5th	
Oulton Park:	6th	4th	11th
TT Circuit Assen:	C	3rd	
Silverstone:	C	10th	
Brands Hatch GP:	7th	7th	6th

Richard Cooper
Anvil Hire TAG Kawasaki/Buildbase BMW Motorrad

Results			
Position:			8th
Points:			156
Qualifying Poles:			0
Fastest Lap Poles:			0
Front Rows:			1
Best Grid:			P3
Races:			23
Wins:			0
Podiums:			2
Best Result:			2nd
Fastest Laps:			0
Donington Park:	10th	17th	
Brands Hatch Indy:	11th	15th	
Oulton Park:	10th	7th	
Snetterton:	10th	12th	
Knockhill:	C	13th	
Brands Hatch GP:	2nd	3rd	
Thruxton:	R	R	
Cadwell Park:	8th	7th	
Oulton Park:	7th	8th	7th
TT Circuit Assen:	6th	4th	
Silverstone:	12th	6th	
Brands Hatch GP:	Inj	Inj	Inj

Richard Cooper again excelled in 2015 and a bit like Josh Brookes it was a tale of two halves, although in his case, there was a little bit more of a twist in the story. Steady results at the start of the season saw the diminutive Nottingham man score points in seven of the opening eight races for the Anvil Hire TAG Team before a brilliant performance at Brands Hatch which saw him tempted by the £50,000 'Dash for Cash' after qualifying on the front row. He declined the challenge and scored two podiums but at the very next round, a couple of DNFs saw him part with the team soon after. Stuart Hicken immediately snapped him up for the Buildbase BMW team and he repaid that faith with a string of top ten results from Cadwell Park onwards. He was in contention for the MCE Rider's Cup, but a nasty qualifying crash in the final round saw him ruled out of action, but nonetheless, he'd put in an impressive performance by anyone's standards.

Peter Hickman
RAF Reserves BMW

Rapidly becoming the best all-rounder what with his MCE BSB experience and his burgeoning road racing prowess, Hickman was a man in demand at the start of the season and great things were expected of the Louth rider in his second season with the RAF Reserves Team. A switch to BMW saw an immediate impact with a superb performance at Donington Park in round one, but a couple of hefty crashes followed in subsequent rounds, one of which at Oulton Park saw him ruled out of the North West 200. A superb performance at the TT saw him then back in BSB action although the results were steady until August came and after a debut Superbike win at the Ulster GP, he made it a month to remember with a double podium at his local Cadwell Park. He scored another podium at Silverstone late in the year by which time his focus was turning to 2016 where once again, he'll be a major contender on both the roads and the short circuits with a new team.

Results			
Position:			9th
Points:			150
Qualifying Poles:			0
Fastest Lap Poles:			0
Front Rows:			2
Best Grid:			P3
Races:			24
Wins:			0
Podiums:			3
Best Result:			2nd
Fastest Laps:			0
Donington Park:	5th	4th	
Brands Hatch Indy:	C	14th	
Oulton Park:	Inj	Inj	
Snetterton:	12th	15th	
Knockhill:	10th	9th	
Brands Hatch GP:	C	13th	
Thruxton:	R	R	
Cadwell Park:	2nd	2nd	
Oulton Park:	10th	6th	R
TT Circuit Assen:	9th	13th	
Silverstone:	3rd	8th	
Brands Hatch GP:	12th	12th	11th

Christian Iddon
Bennetts Suzuki

If winning championships came down to grit and determination, Christian Iddon would have won hands down in 2015 after what can only be described as a contrasting season. On the back of a season in World Superbikes, the multiple British Supermoto champion signed for the Bennetts Suzuki team and was immediately on the pace. Then came Brands Hatch where he broke his leg in race one and raced to 12th in race two. That injury affected him more than most realised, but he plugged away only for another big crash at Thruxton, which set him back further. But Iddon did what he does best and in the face of adversity, he finished the last four rounds strongly, never out of the top ten. Indeed, just how he missed out on a podium in the final couple of Showdown rounds is one of life's mysteries, but a top ten in his return to the UK was a brilliant result, all things considered.

Results			
Position:			10th
Points:			146
Qualifying Poles:			0
Fastest Lap Poles:			0
Front Rows:			1
Best Grid:			P3
Races:			26
Wins:			0
Podiums:			0
Best Result:			4th
Fastest Laps:			0
Donington Park:	7th	5th	
Brands Hatch Indy:	C	12th	
Oulton Park:	17th	15th	
Snetterton:	16th	9th	
Knockhill:	R	10th	
Brands Hatch GP:	13th	8th	
Thruxton:	C	20th	
Cadwell Park:	9th	13th	
Oulton Park:	C	9th	8th
TT Circuit Assen:	7th	6th	
Silverstone:	8th	4th	
Brands Hatch GP:	4th	8th	5th

1st	Finishing Position	R	Retired
C	Crashed	Inj.	Injured

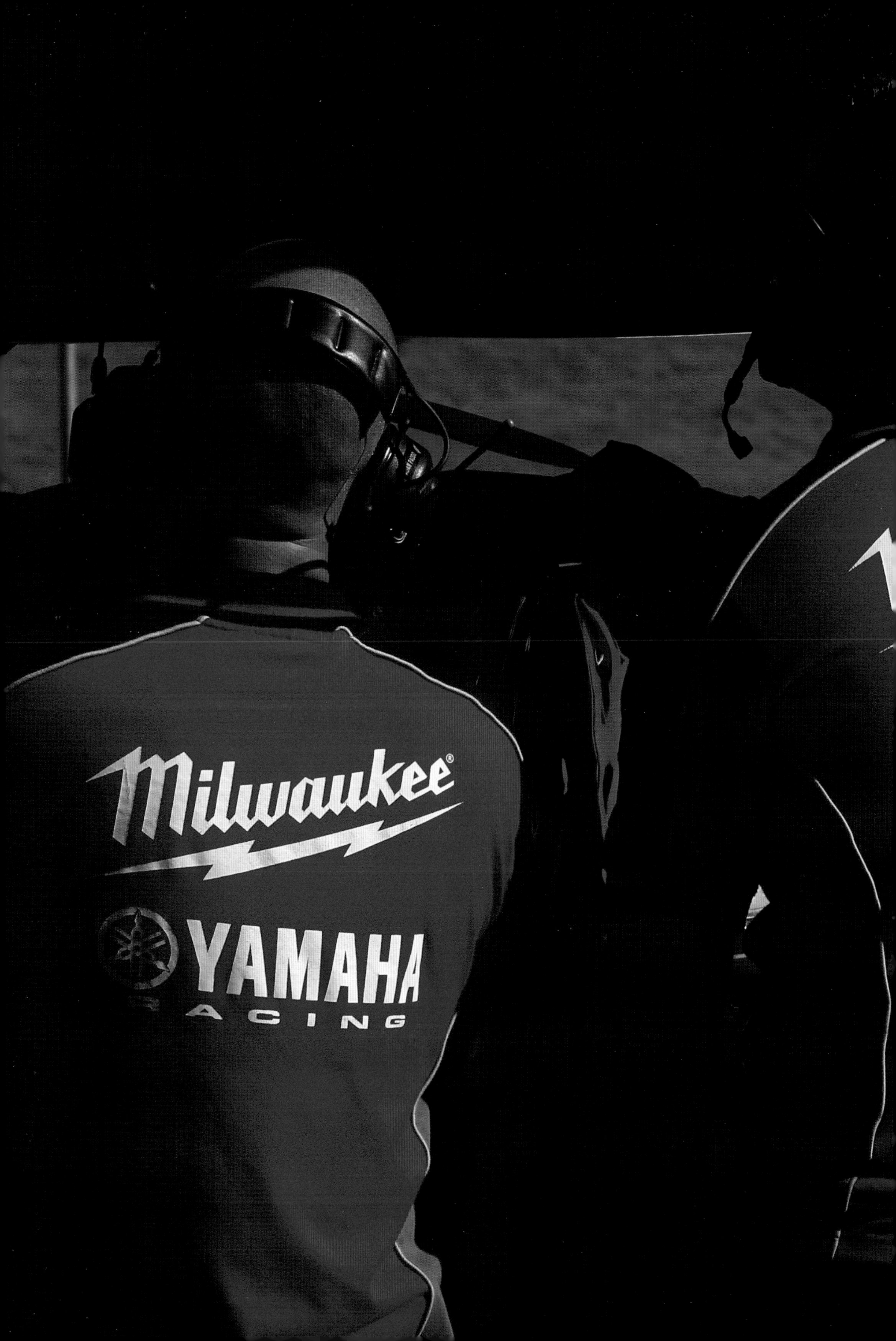
Milwaukee
YAMAHA
RACING

Milwaukee Yamaha

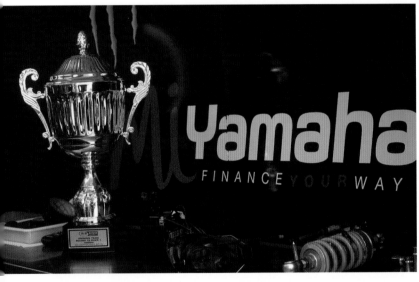

Milwaukee Yamaha

Machinery: Yamaha YZF-R1
Owner: Shaun Muir
Located: Guisborough, Cleveland
Pedigree: MCE British Superbike Champions 2011 & 2015
Website: www.milwaukeeyamaha.com

After going ten races without a win at the start of the season aboard the brand new YZF-R1, the second half of the year was a tale of virtual domination with Josh Brookes winning 13 out of the last 16 races to become a worthy MCE BSB champion at his seventh attempt. His only blot in a near perfect season was a crash in the final race long after he'd wrapped up the title but it mattered not. Initial team-mate Broc Parkes struggled in the early stages and parted with the team mid-season with riders including Adam Jenkinson and latterly Jakub Smrz deputising for Shaun Muir's team.

Josh Brookes	
Number:	25
From:	Bringelly, New South Wales, Australia
First BSB Race:	Brands Hatch 2009
MCE BSB Races:	172
MCE BSB Wins:	33
MCE BSB Podiums:	66
MCE BSB Poles:	35
Honours:	Double Australian Champion 2005 MCE BSB Champion 2015

Jakub Smrz	
Number:	96
From:	Ceske Budejovice, Czech Republic
First BSB Race:	Assen, 2012
MCE BSB Races:	64
MCE BSB Wins:	0
MCE BSB Podiums:	0
MCE BSB Poles:	1
Honours:	Five World Superbike Championship podiums

Other riders: Broc Parkes, Adam Jenkinson

PBM Be Wiser Kawasaki

PBM Be Wiser Kawasaki

Machinery: Kawasaki ZX-10R
Owner: Paul Bird
Located: Penrith, Cumbria
Pedigree: MCE British Superbike Champions 2002, 2003, 2012 & 2014
Website: www.pbmuk.net

The opening rounds saw Shane Byrne looking favourite to challenge for an unprecedented fifth MCE BSB crown, but the second half of the season saw the defending champion's challenge stall as an uncharacteristic lean spell put him and the team on the back foot. Try as he might, he had no answer for Brookes and despite a valiant attempt at the final round, he had to hand his crown over to his bitter rival. Team-mate Stuart Easton's season was wrecked through injury at the halfway stage after a promising first half which had seen him take a win at Oulton Park.

Stuart Easton	
Number:	5
From:	Hawick, Scotland
First BSB Race:	Silverstone 2004
MCE BSB Races:	144
MCE BSB Wins:	4
MCE BSB Podiums:	25
MCE BSB Poles:	1
Honours:	British Supersport Champion 2002 & 2013, four Macau GP wins

Shane Byrne	
Number:	67
From:	Sittingbourne, Kent
First BSB Race:	Silverstone 1999
MCE BSB Races:	297
MCE BSB Wins:	68
MCE BSB Podiums:	89
MCE BSB Poles:	42
Honours:	Four-times MCE BSB Champion 2003, 2008, 2012 & 2014

Other riders: Danny Buchan, Ian Hutchinson

PIT-LANE

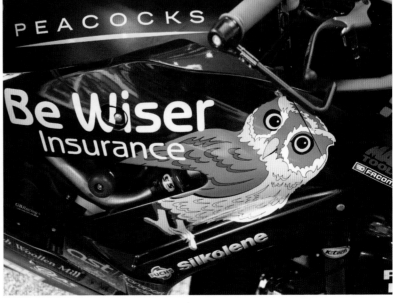

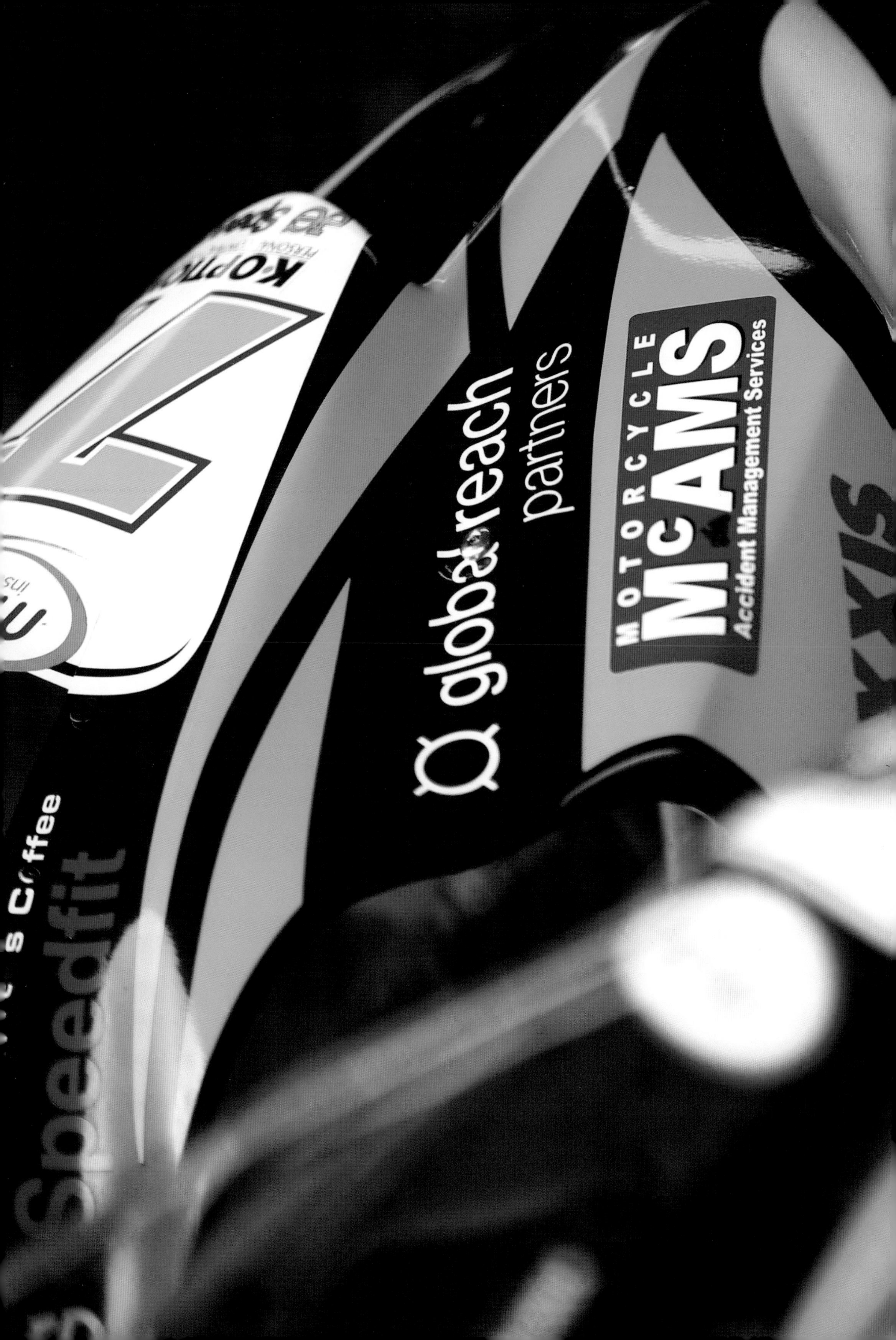
partners
MOTORCYCLE
McAMS
Accident Management Services
Speedfit

JG Speedfit
Kawasaki

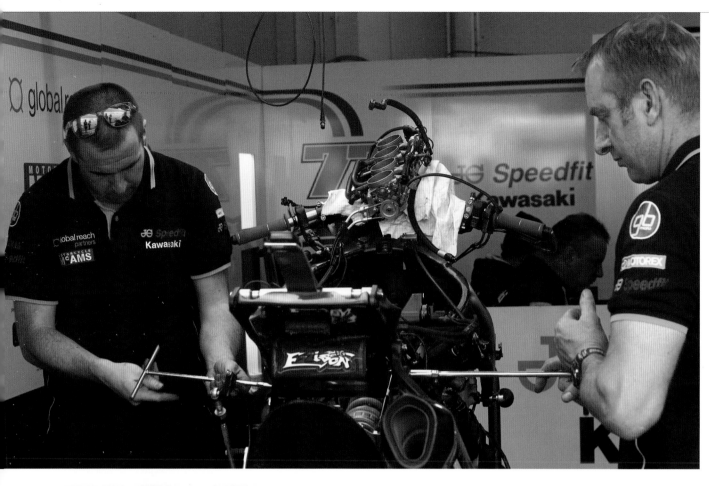

JG Speedfit Kawasaki

Machinery: Kawasaki ZX-10R
Principal: Mark Smith-Halvorsen
Located: Felbridge, West Sussex
Pedigree: MCE BSB race winners
Website: www.gbmoto.com

James Ellison was hoping that 2015 would be his best shot at the title, especially after an encouraging start to the season which saw him win two of the opening three races to lead the championship early on. But then the Ellison jinx struck and a nasty fall at Snetterton was followed by a broken wrist at Thruxton and despite a late push in the Showdown, his title hopes disappeared when grip issues saw him score no points in race two at Silverstone. James Westmoreland took a podium at Thruxton but split with the team at Assen whereafter they fielded British Supersport champion Luke Stapleford for the last two rounds.

James Ellison	
Number:	77
From:	Kendal, Cumbria
First BSB Race:	Silverstone 2004
MCE BSB Races:	174
MCE BSB Wins:	12
MCE BSB Podiums:	37
MCE BSB Poles:	7
Honours:	Double European Superstock & World Endurance Champion

James Westmoreland	
Number:	6
From:	Hull, East Yorkshire
First BSB Race:	Brands Hatch 2011
MCE BSB Races:	112
MCE BSB Wins:	0
MCE BSB Podiums:	1
MCE BSB Poles:	2
Honours:	Three times British Supersport Championship runner-up

Other rider: Luke Stapleford

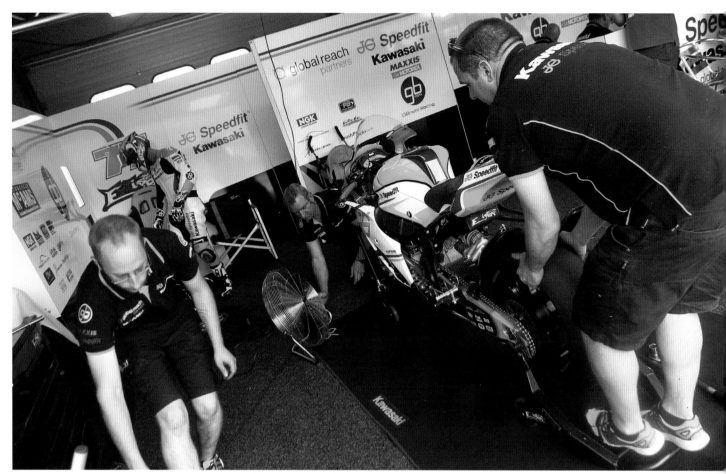

Tyco BMW Motorrad

Tyco BMW Motorrad

Machinery: BMW S1000RR
Manager: Philip Neill
Located: Moneymore, Northern Ireland
Pedigree: Motorpoint British Supersport & Superstock Champions
Website: www.tycobmw.com

Another team with a brand new model for 2015 in the shape of the new BMW of which great things were expected. The only team to get two riders into the Showdown but neither Tommy Bridewell nor Michael Laverty could muster a serious challenge to lift the 2015 MCE BSB crown. Laverty plugged away all season and found some pace towards the end of the year with three podiums and a win in the Showdown. After flashes of brilliance during the season, it's a case of what might have been for Bridewell who sensationally won at Oulton Park in May but proved a little inconsistent at other times.

Tommy Bridewell	
Number:	46
From:	Devizes, Wiltshire
First BSB Race:	Brands Hatch 2007
MCE BSB Races:	174
MCE BSB Wins:	2
MCE BSB Podiums:	13
MCE BSB Poles:	1
Honours:	Third 2014 MCE BSB Championship

Michael Laverty	
Number:	7
From:	Toome, County Antrim
First BSB Race:	Silverstone 2004
MCE BSB Races:	173
MCE BSB Wins:	8
MCE BSB Podiums:	25
MCE BSB Poles:	5
Honours:	British Supersport Champion 2007

Honda Racing

Honda Racing

Dan Linfoot

Number:	4
From:	Wetherby, North Yorkshire
First BSB Race:	Silverstone 2009
MCE BSB Races:	125
MCE BSB Wins:	0
MCE BSB Podiums:	5
MCE BSB Poles:	2
Honours:	European Championship and 125/250cc Grand Prix experience

Jenny Tinmouth

Number:	20
From:	Ellesmere Port, Cheshire
First BSB Race:	Croft 2011
MCE BSB Races:	93
MCE BSB Wins:	0
MCE BSB Podiums:	0
MCE BSB Poles:	0
Honours:	Fastest lady TT rider, first lady to score MCE BSB points

Jason O'Halloran

Number:	22
From:	Wollongong, Australia
First BSB Race:	Croft 2008
MCE BSB Races:	33
MCE BSB Wins:	0
MCE BSB Podiums:	2
MCE BSB Poles:	0
Honours:	Australian Supersport Champion 2007

Other rider: Julien Da Costa

Machinery: Honda CBR1000RR Fireblade
Manager: Havier Beltran
Located: Louth, Lincolnshire
Pedigree: MCE British Superbike Champions 2006, 2007, 2010 & 2013
Website: www.honda-racing.co.uk

After a brilliant start to the season, which was soon scuppered by a broken wrist, Dan Linfoot combined results good and bad to secure his Showdown place in the final race of the main season. A podium at Silverstone was as good as it got in his bid for the championship but in all fairness, Dan will be the first to admit he under-achieved this year. Team-mate Jason O'Halloran scored a double podium at Snetterton before a broken leg ruled him out from Thruxton onwards and Jenny Tinmouth did a great job for the team, but wasn't able to score any points in her first season as a factory rider.

Buildbase BMW
Motorrad

Buildbase BMW Motorrad

Machinery: BMW S1000RR
Owner: Stuart Hicken
Located: Peggs Green, Leicestershire
Pedigree: MCE British Superbike race winners
Website: www.buildbasebmw.co.uk

After such a great showing in 2014 whereby he just missed out on the MCE BSB title after a crash in the final round at Brands Hatch, and a strong start to 2015, it all went wrong for former triple champion Ryuichi Kiyonari following a crash at Oulton Park in May. He never found his true form thereafter and parted with the team before the final round. Lee Jackson gave a good account of himself in his first full season as a model of consistency and likewise Richard Cooper, who joined the team mid-season, but a big crash in qualifying for the last round ended his season a day early.

Ryuichi Kiyonari

Number:	23
From:	Saitama, Japan
First BSB Race:	Silverstone 2004
MCE BSB Races:	217
MCE BSB Wins:	50
MCE BSB Podiums:	44
MCE BSB Poles:	18
Honours:	Triple British Superbike Champion, 2006, 2007 & 2010

Lee Jackson

Number:	14
From:	Lincoln
First BSB Race:	Brands Hatch 2014
MCE BSB Races:	35
MCE BSB Wins:	0
MCE BSB Podiums:	0
MCE BSB Poles:	0
Honours:	National Superstock 600 Champion 2012

Richard Cooper

Number:	47
From:	Nottingham
First BSB Race:	Mallory Park, 2009
MCE BSB Races:	36
MCE BSB Wins:	0
MCE BSB Podiums:	3
MCE BSB Poles:	0
Honours:	National Superstock Champion 2011, BSB-EVO race winner

SUZUKI

TEAM

UKI

Bennetts

Bennetts Suzuki

Bennetts Suzuki

Machinery: Suzuki GSX-R 1000
Owner: Martin Halsall
Located: Bolton, Lancashire
Pedigree: MCE BSB podium finishers
Website: www.halsallracingteam.co.uk

The Bennetts Suzuki team gave a good account of themselves this season, which culminated with Christian Iddon nearly scoring a podium in the final two rounds where he was challenging the established front-runners. The Supermoto ace showed great pace throughout the season, but coupled with some high speed crashes in which he hurt himself, it meant he finished lower down the standings than he should have. Aussie team-mate Josh Waters again found the going tough and could only manage a best result of 10th at Thruxton.

Josh Waters	
Number:	21
From:	Mildura, Victoria, Australia
First BSB Race:	Brands Hatch 2013
MCE BSB Races:	78
MCE BSB Wins:	2
MCE BSB Podiums:	1
MCE BSB Poles:	2
Honours:	Double Australian Superbike Champion 2009 & 2012

Christian Iddon	
Number:	24
From:	Stockport, Greater Manchester
First BSB Race:	Brands Hatch 2010
MCE BSB Races:	38
MCE BSB Wins:	0
MCE BSB Podiums:	0
MCE BSB Poles:	1
Honours:	10 times ACU/British Supermoto Champion

Be Wiser Kawasaki

Machinery: Kawasaki ZX-10R
Owner: Alan Greig
Located: Lincoln
Pedigree: MCE BSB Podium Finishers
Website: www.bewiserkawasaki.co.uk

After a 2015 season of contrasting fortunes for both Danny Buchan and veteran team-mate Chris Walker, it all came good at Oulton Park in September as Buchan claimed a maiden double podium which he'd been threatening to do for a while had it not been for some hefty crashes. Walker's was a season of frustration, although he did throw in the odd good result, but following the departure of Manager Tommy Hill earlier in the season, the team announced they were withdrawing from the series following Assen.

Chris Walker

Number:	9
From:	Ollerton, Nottinghamshire
First BSB Race:	Donington Park, 1996
MCE BSB Races:	304
MCE BSB Wins:	21
MCE BSB Podiums:	51
MCE BSB Poles:	11
Honours:	4 x runner-up British Superbike Championship

Danny Buchan

Number:	83
From:	Burnham on Crouch, Essex
First BSB Race:	Brands Hatch 2012
MCE BSB Races:	45
MCE BSB Wins:	0
MCE BSB Podiums:	2
MCE BSB Poles:	0
Honours:	2014 National Superstock 1000 Champion

Quattro Plant Bournemouth Kawasaki

Quattro Plant Bournemouth Kawasaki

Machinery: Kawasaki ZX-10R
Owner: Peter Extance
Located: Bournemouth, Dorset
Pedigree: MCE BSB race winners
Website: www.quattroplantkawasaki.co.uk

After a steady start for both Luke Mossey and Howie Mainwaring Smart, they soon started to make their presence felt with some impressive performances. Howie was a regular top ten finisher in the opening rounds before a frustrating second half of the season, whereas conversely, Mossey started his rookie season steadily before becoming a force to be reckoned with as the year progressed. The fact that Mossey scored two podiums and clinched the MCE Rider's Cup was testament to his skill and the ability of the team.

Luke Mossey	
Number:	12
From:	Cambridge
First BSB Race:	Donington Park, 2015
MCE BSB Races:	26
MCE BSB Wins:	0
MCE BSB Podiums:	2
MCE BSB Poles:	0
Honours:	MCE Rider's Cup Champion 2015

Howie Mainwaring Smart	
Number:	43
From:	Frodsham, Cheshire
First BSB Race:	Donington Park, 2005
MCE BSB Races:	120
MCE BSB Wins:	1
MCE BSB Podiums:	1
MCE BSB Poles:	0
Honours:	4th National Superstock 1000 Championship 2010

Anvil Hire TAG
Racing Kawasaki

Anvil Hire TAG Racing Kawasaki

Machinery: Kawasaki ZX-10R
Owner: Rob Winfield
Located: Swadlincote, Derbyshire
Pedigree: MCE BSB podium finishers
Website: www.tagracing.co.uk

It's a case of what might have been for the Midlands-based team with amiable Swedish rider Filip Backlund and young British team-mate Shaun Winfield. Backlund didn't show his true potential this year, whereas Winfield continued to gain experience in MCE BSB. Prior to leaving the team, Richard Cooper scored a couple of podiums at Brands Hatch in midsummer proving the bike and the team to be capable of success but sadly neither Backlund nor Winfield looked like repeating that.

Shaun Winfield

Number:	8
From:	Swadlincote, Derbyshire
First BSB Race:	Oulton Park, 2014
MCE BSB Races:	35
MCE BSB Wins:	0
MCE BSB Podiums:	0
MCE BSB Poles:	0
Honours:	British Championship points scorer

Filip Backlund

Number:	99
From:	Vasteras, Sweden
First BSB Race:	Donington Park 2014
MCE BSB Races:	31
MCE BSB Wins:	0
MCE BSB Podiums:	0
MCE BSB Poles:	0
Honours:	Swedish Pro-Superbike Champion 2011

Other Rider: Richard Cooper

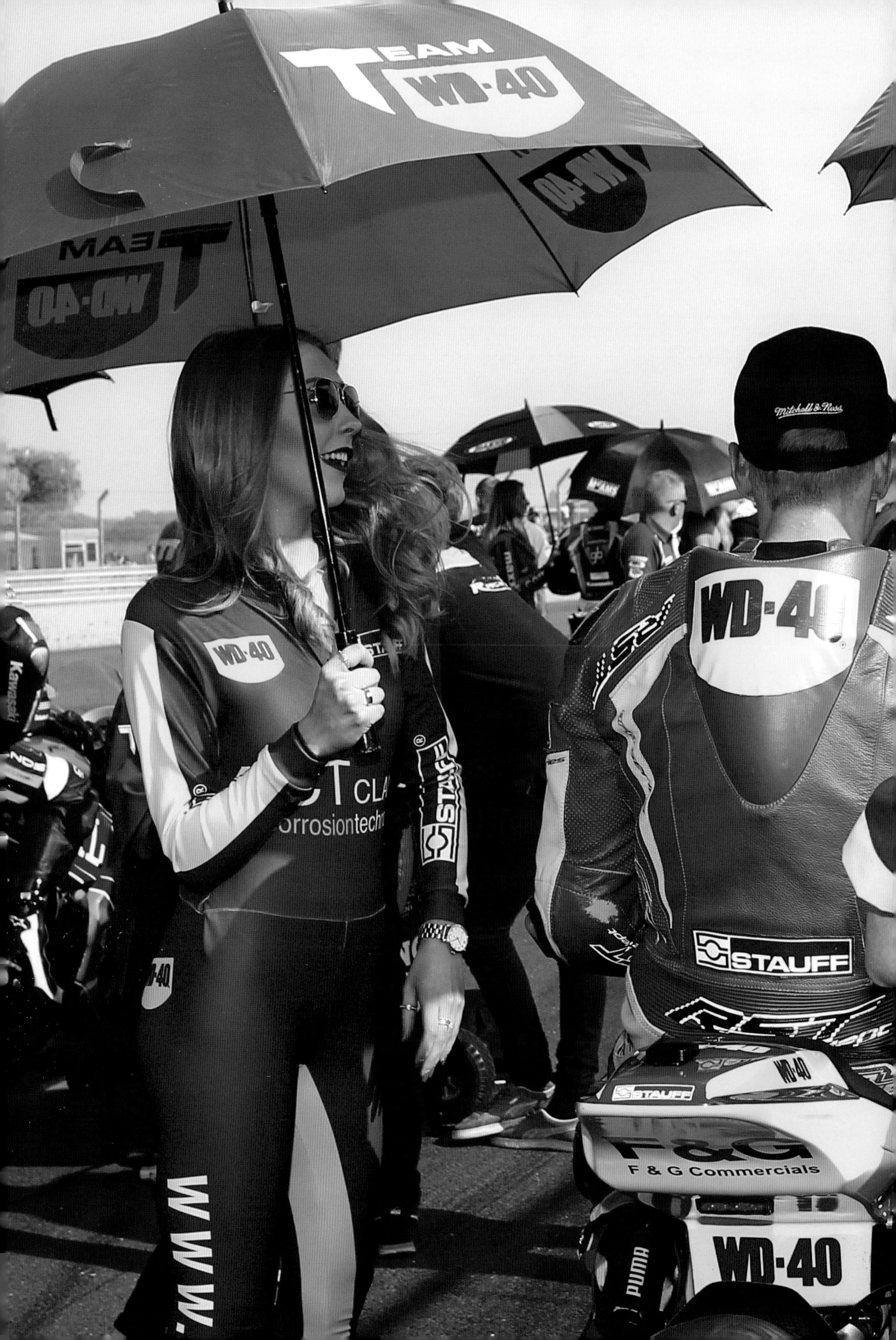
TEAM
WD-40
STAUFF
F&G
F & G Commercials
WD-40
PUMA

Team WD-40 Kawasaki

Team WD-40 Kawasaki

Machinery: Kawasaki ZX-10R
Owner: Brent Gladwin
Located: Sheffield, South Yorkshire
Pedigree: Debut season in MCE BSB
Website: www.grmotosport.co.uk

Following a frustrating first half of the season, former World Supersport exile Jack Kennedy started to rack up the performances from mid-season onwards only to be thwarted by injury later in the season which halted his progress. For former 125cc GP racer Taylor Mackenzie, it was a season of frustration and he enjoyed very little luck just missing out on the points on a number of occasions. His moment in the spotlight came when he had to leap from his blazing bike mid-race at Snetterton when it caught fire!

Taylor Mackenzie

Number:	11
From:	Ashby-de-la-Zouch, Leicestershire
First BSB Race:	Donington Park, 2015
MCE BSB Races:	23
MCE BSB Wins:	0
MCE BSB Podiums:	0
MCE BSB Poles:	0
Honours:	4th 2010 British 125cc Championship Grand Prix experience

Jack Kennedy

Number:	44
From:	Dublin, Ireland
First BSB Race:	Donington Park, 2015
MCE BSB Races:	23
MCE BSB Wins:	0
MCE BSB Podiums:	0
MCE BSB Poles:	0
Honours:	Runner-up 2012 British Supersport Championship

RAF Reserves BMW

Machinery: BMW S1000RR
Manager: Lee Hardy
Located: RAF Marham, Norfolk
Pedigree: Race winners in MCE BSB
Website: www.raf.mod.co.uk

After a great start to the season whereby he just missed out on a podiu at Donington Park, it was a contrasting season for Peter Hickman wh with an injury and some technical problems coupled with some gre rides. Those included a double podium at his local Cadwell Park a he sampled more silverware at Silverstone. Hickman also excelled the roads despite missing the NW200 through injury but won at t Ulster GP.

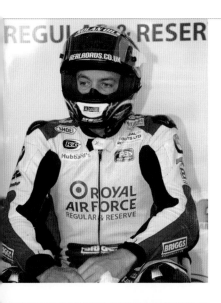

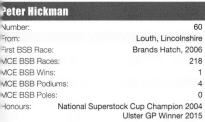

Peter Hickman	
Number:	60
From:	Louth, Lincolnshire
First BSB Race:	Brands Hatch, 2006
MCE BSB Races:	218
MCE BSB Wins:	1
MCE BSB Podiums:	4
MCE BSB Poles:	0
Honours:	National Superstock Cup Champion 2004
	Ulster GP Winner 2015

Riders Motorcycles BMW

Machinery: BMW S1000RR
Principal: Phil Jessopp
Located: Bridgwater, Somerset
Pedigree: MCE British Superbike & NW200 race winners
Website: www.ridersmotorcycles.com

2015 was a season of two halves for Martin Jessopp who only managed three points scoring rides in the opening six meetings. Following on, he found a new lease of life scoring good points and qualifying well, but although the results tailed off towards the end of the year, he still was a regular points scorer.

Martin Jessopp

Number:	40
From:	Yeovil, Somerset
First BSB Race:	Brands Hatch, 2008
MCE BSB Races:	147
MCE BSB Wins:	0
MCE BSB Podiums:	0
MCE BSB Poles:	1
Honours:	Runner-up British Superbike Cup 2008

Morello Racing Kawasaki

Machinery: Kawasaki ZX-10R
Principal: Steve Buckenham
Located: Norwich, Norfolk
Pedigree: Second season in MCE BSB
Website: www.morelloservices.co.uk

After a debut season in 2014, which included some encouraging results, the team expanded to MCE BSB and this season saw a number of riders take up the challenge. The team's former Pirelli Superstock 1000 rider John Ingram was the rider in the saddle for the last few rounds and he gave a good account of himself although couldn't scrape into the points.

John Ingram

Number:	56
From:	Wigan, Lancs
First BSB Race:	Donington Park, 2007
MCE BSB Races:	35
MCE BSB Wins:	0
MCE BSB Podiums:	0
MCE BSB Poles:	0
Honours:	Multiple club racing champion

Other Riders: Victor Cox, Danny Johnson, Lee Costello, David McFadden

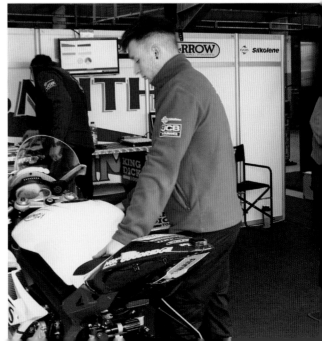

Smiths Racing BMW

Machinery: BMW S1000RR
Owner / Manager: Alan Smith/Rebecca Smith
Located: Gloucester
Pedigree: Double British Supersport Champions and TT winners
Website: www.smithsracing.co.uk

The double Motorpoint British Supersport champions made the step up to MCE BSB with reigning champion Billy McConnell aboard the brand new BMW. The Australian was largely impressive this term scoring regular points which was highlighted with a superb podium at Cadwell Park and to end up in the top 15 of the series was a major achievement for both rider and team.

Billy McConnell

Number:	3
From:	Adelaide, South Australia
First BSB Race:	Brands Hatch 2006
MCE BSB Races:	74
MCE BSB Wins:	0
MCE BSB Podiums:	1
MCE BSB Poles:	0
Honours:	2014 British Supersport Champion

Lloyds British Moto Rapido Ducati

Machinery: Ducati 1199 Panigale
Owner: Steve Moore
Located: Winchester, Hampshire
Pedigree: Race winners in BSB-EVO
Website: www.motorapido.co.uk

Flamboyant Anglo-American John Hopkins joined the team in mid-season after Jakub Smrz was ruled out with injury and immediately showed his class and the Panigale's potential with a top six in his first race at Brands Hatch. Thereafter, a series of technical problems thwarted his bid, but a superb podium place in the final round made up for the disappointments.

John Hopkins

Number:	15
From:	San Diego, California, USA
First BSB Race:	Brands Hatch, 2011
MCE BSB Races:	64
MCE BSB Wins:	5
MCE BSB Podiums:	12
MCE BSB Poles:	4
Honours:	Triple AMA Champion, 4th 2007 MotoGP World Championship

Other Rider: Jakub Smrz

A Plant Yamaha

Machinery: Yamaha YZF-R1
Manager: Neil Bamford
Located: Loughborough, Leicestershire
Pedigree: Points scorers in MCE BSB

One of the best privateers in the business, the experienced Aaron Zanotti took the brave step to campaign the brand new Yamaha R1. As a result, the season was very much about developing the machine and he did a brilliant job despite some technical issues although just missed out on scoring points.

Aaron Zanotti	
Number:	64
From:	Loughborough, Leicestershire
First BSB Race:	Brands Hatch, 2007
MCE BSB Races:	211
MCE BSB Wins:	0
MCE BSB Podiums:	0
MCE BSB Poles:	0
Honours:	Runner-up National Superstock Championship 2006

SBK City
Kawasaki

Machinery: Kawasaki ZX-10R
Principal: Rhalf Lo Turco
Located: London E1
Pedigree: Second season in MCE BSB
Website: www.sbkcity.co.uk

The cosmopolitan rider from Sao Paulo made history by becoming the first Brazilian to race in MCE BSB last season and continued to add more international flavour to this year's series. Rhalf didn't enjoy the best of starts with a number of heavy crashes, and showed good pace at times but couldn't trouble the scoreboard.

Rhalf Lo Turco	
Number:	45
From:	Sao Paulo, Brazil
First BSB Race:	Brands Hatch, 2014
MCE BSB Races:	39
MCE BSB Wins:	0
MCE BSB Podiums:	0
MCE BSB Poles:	0
Honours:	Club Champion & World Endurance experience

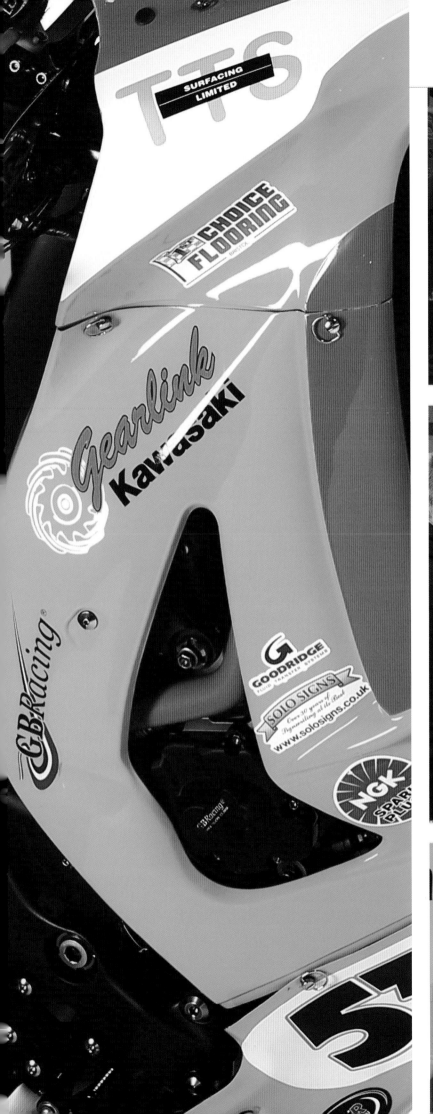

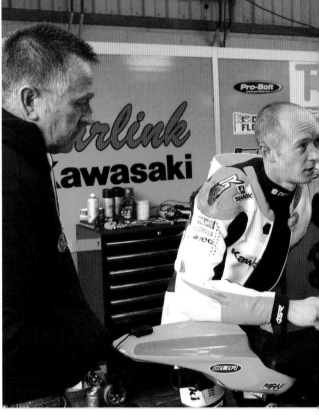

Gearlink Kawasaki

Machinery: Kawasaki ZX-10R
Owner: Michael and Norma de Bidaph
Located: Salisbury, Wiltshire
Pedigree: Second season in MCE BSB
Website: www.gearlinkracing.com

The family team from Wiltshire has endured a frustrating time of things since making the move up to MCE BSB whereby they admirably persevered with the development of their ZX-10R. After a number of riders graced the seat this season, Jed Metcher was the pick of the bunch, although the last rider entrusted with the machine, James Westmoreland, gave a good account of himself in the final round.

Jed Metcher	
Number:	71
From:	Melbourne, Victoria, Australia
First BSB Race:	Assen, 2014
MCE BSB Races:	20
MCE BSB Wins:	0
MCE BSB Podiums:	0
MCE BSB Poles:	0
Honours:	2011 European Superstock 600 Champion

Other riders: Joe Burns, Michael Rutter, Victor Cox, Barry Burrell, James Westmoreland

Above: Robbin Harms

Top middle: Joe Burns

Top right: Jed Metcher

Below: Danny Johnson

Bottom middle: James Rose

Bottom right: Vittorio Iannuzzo

Supporting Cast

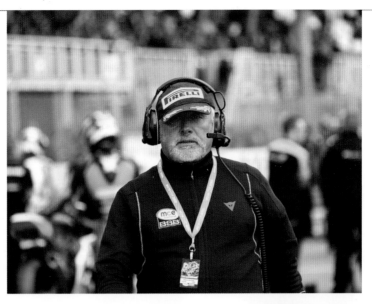

www.ttcircuit.com

Circuit Maps

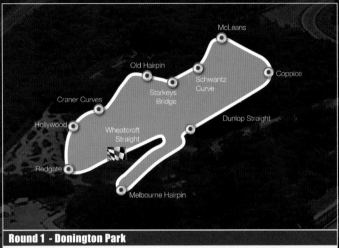

Round 1 - Donington Park

Circuit length - 2.4873m (4.0029km)

Shane Byrne (Kawasaki) 2015 - 1:29.512

Round 2 - Brands Hatch Indy

Circuit length - 1.2079m (1.944km)

James Ellison (Kawasaki) 2015 - 45.212

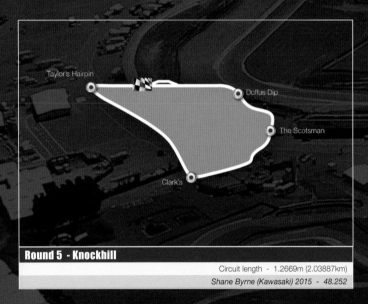

Round 5 - Knockhill

Circuit length - 1.2669m (2.03887km)

Shane Byrne (Kawasaki) 2015 - 48.252

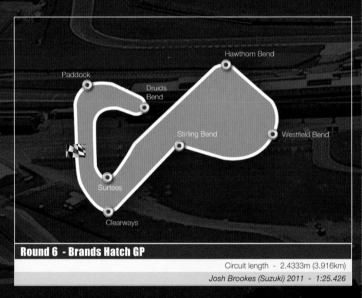

Round 6 - Brands Hatch GP

Circuit length - 2.4333m (3.916km)

Josh Brookes (Suzuki) 2011 - 1:25.426

Round 9 - Oulton Park

Circuit length - 2.6920m (4.332km)

Josh Brookes (Yamaha) 2015 - 1:34.483

Round 10 - TT Circuit Assen

Circuit length - 2.822m (4.542km)

Josh Brookes (Yamaha) 2015 - 1:36.904

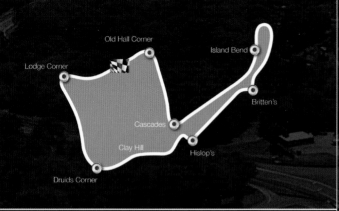

Round 3 - Oulton Park

Old Hall Corner
Island Bend
Lodge Corner
Britten's
Cascades
Clay Hill
Hislop's
Druids Corner

Circuit length - 2.6920m (4.332km)

Shane Byrne (Kawasaki) 2015 - 1:35.007

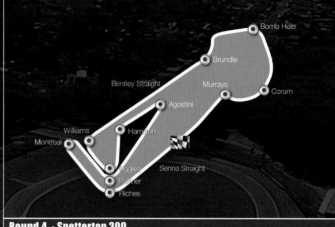

Round 4 - Snetterton 300

Bomb Hole
Brundle
Bentley Straight
Murrays
Coram
Agostini
Williams
Hamilton
Montreal
Oggies
Senna Straight
Palmer
Riches

Circuit length - 2.96m (4.763km)

Josh Brookes (Yamaha) 2014 - 1:47.882

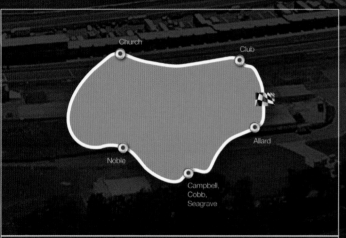

Round 7 - Thruxton

Church
Club
Allard
Noble
Campbell, Cobb, Seagrave

Circuit length - 2.3560m (3.79161km)

Josh Brookes (Yamaha) 2015 - 1:14.884

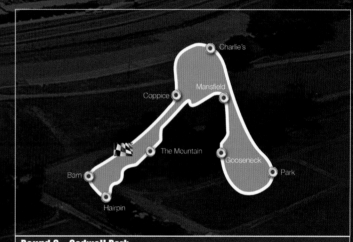

Round 8 - Cadwell Park

Charlie's
Mansfield
Coppice
The Mountain
Gooseneck
Park
Barn
Hairpin

Circuit length - 2.1800m (3.508km)

Leon Haslam (Ducati) 2007 - 1:26.654

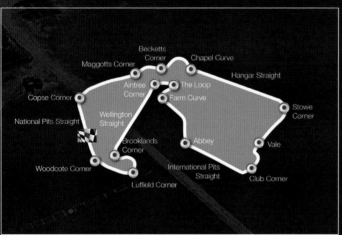

Round 11 - Silverstone Arena GP

Becketts Corner
Chapel Curve
Maggotts Corner
Hangar Straight
Aintree Corner
The Loop
Copse Corner
Farm Curve
Stowe Corner
Wellington Straight
National Pits Straight
Brooklands Corner
Abbey
Vale
Woodcote Corner
International Pits Straight
Club Corner
Luffield Corner

Circuit length - 3.6673m (5.901km)

James Ellison (Kawasaki) 2015 - 2:05.267

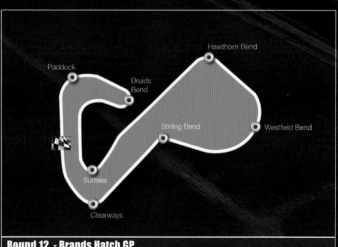

Round 12 - Brands Hatch GP

Hawthorn Bend
Paddock
Druids Bend
Stirling Bend
Westfield Bend
Surtees
Clearways

Circuit length - 2.4333m (3.916km)

Josh Brookes (Suzuki) 2011 - 1:25.426

01

Donington Park

04 - 06 APRIL 2015

Top: Byrne gets off to a flying start

Centre: Linfoot kept Byrne honest

Top right: It's a PBM 1-2 as Easton gets off to a strong start behind team-mate Shane 'Shakey' Byrne

Bottom left: 'Old but Gold' Chris Walker began his umpteenth season in BSB on the Be Wiser Kawasaki

Bottom right: Ellison started his season in winning ways before a flat battery saw him start from the back of the grid in race two

Top left: Brookes gets his head down on his way to two solid finishes on the all new Milwaukee Yamaha R1

Top: Dan Linfoot showed good speed as he heads Byrne and Easton

Left: Broc Parkes took a tumble at Goddards

Bottom left: Supersport champ Billy 'Skippy' McConnell and Superstock 1000 champ Danny Buchan made the step into the Superbike class for 2015

Below: Ellison heads Byrne

Left: Ellison catches O'Halloran as he fights his way through the pack after starting from the back of the grid

Right: Shakey on the limit as he gives it "The Doctor's Dangle' into Redgate

Bottom left: Ellison takes the race win ahead of reigning champion Byrne

Bottom right: Brookes hard on the gas out of the Melbourne Loop

ELLISON AND BYRNE SHARE OPENING SPOILS

A new season and new challenges, but for the four-time title winning Shane 'Shakey' Byrne it was to be a painful beginning as a month on from a big tumble in Spanish testing and an operation to pin and plate a broken hand, not forgetting an ankle injury, he had a job to do.

He put his PBM Kawasaki on the front row alongside James Ellison while Ryuichi Kiyonari, eager to set the record straight after his last round tumble of the previous season had cost him a chance of a fourth crown, took pole.

In the season opener, Byrne grabbed the lead, followed by JG Speedfit Kawasaki's Ellison and PBM team-mate Stuart Easton while Kiyonari faltered with a tardy getaway, but after a Safety Car intervention following Rhalf Lo Turco's crash, Ellison turned up the power, roared into the lead and despite the best efforts of Byrne, there was no stopping him taking the win.

Brookes ran third for Milwaukee Yamaha ahead of Honda Racing's Dan Linfoot, giving the Louth based team some joy on their full-time return to the series as their other riders struggled. Jason O'Halloran finished back in 19th while Jenny Tinmouth crashed for a second time that weekend.

Ellison was left rueing his luck when a flat battery ruled him out of the sighting lap for the second race and ensured a back of the grid start. However, the Cumbrian fought all of the way, salvaging a handful of points but was never in with a chance of victory. Byrne seized the opportunity, though Linfoot countered him, and it was not until three laps from the end at the Old Hairpin that Byrne made the decisive move to take the win ahead of the Honda rider with Stuart Easton third. Peter Hickman completed a strong all-round showing on the RAF Reserves Honda in fourth while Christian Iddon brought the Bennetts Suzuki home ahead of sixth placed Brookes, who lost time avoiding a crashing Kiyo.

The series began with a healthy 35 bikes on the grid, but for some of the newcomers it was a tough baptism. Danny Buchan, graduating as the National Superstock 1000 champion, showed pace but crashed. Billy McConnell, the British Supersport title winner bounced back from a first race tumble to earn points for the Smiths BMW team as he ran ninth while Taylor Mackenzie was plagued by machine problems.

RACE 1	(20 LAPS)
1 ELLISON	JG Speedfit Kawasaki
2 BYRNE	PBM Kawasaki
3 BROOKES	Milwaukee Yamaha

RACE 2	(20 LAPS)
1 BYRNE	PBM Kawasaki
2 LINFOOT	Honda Racing
3 EASTON	PBM Kawasaki

BSB CHAMPIONSHIP POINTS		PP
1 BYRNE	45	8
2 LINFOOT	33	3
3 ELLISON	29	5
4 BROOKES	26	1
5 HICKMAN	24	0
6 EASTON	21	1

02
Brands Hatch
Indy

17 - 19 April 2015

Top: Easton leads Bridewell and Mainwaring Smart

Top right: A packed Brands Hatch grid

Far right: JG Speedfit rider James Ellison was on fire all weekend, here leading Byrne, Brookes and Kiyonari

Right: Tommy Bridewell had a mixed weekend

Left: Parkes leads Smrz, Bridewell and Mainwaring Smart through Paddock Hill bend

Above: Peter Hickman took the Racing RAF Reserves BMW for an excursion into the gravel trap

Top right: Ellison leads the pack through Graham Hill Bend on lap one

Below: Hickman, Parkes, Kennedy, Iddon and Walker in the heat of battle

Bottom right: Three-time BSB champion, Ryuichi Kiyonari pushing reigning champion Shane Byrne

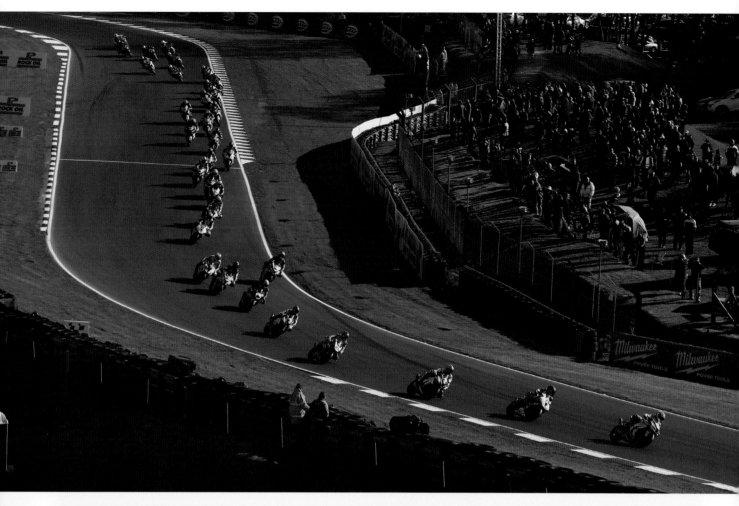

Top left: Taylor Mackenzie on the WD-40 machine leads Kiyonari

Top right: James Westmoreland was on the JG Speedfit Kawasaki

Bottom right: Kiyo chases Byrne

Centre: Tommy Bridewell kicked up some dust at Druids as he crashed out

Below: Tyco BMW team-mate Michael Laverty returned from the MotoGP scene

ELLISON'S PERFECT DAY

For James Ellison, this was to be the best round of his MCE BSB career. A pole position start, the lap record and a first ever series double, the JG Speedfit Kawasaki rider ruled supreme and not even Shane Byrne on his home circuit had any answer to the Cumbrian.

Ellison made the perfect start in race one with Ryuichi Kiyonari hot on the charge aboard his Buildbase BMW as Byrne stuck with them in third place ahead of his PBM Kawasaki team-mate Stuart Easton and Josh Brookes just behind.

The race was reaching its closing stages when first Tommy Bridewell and then Peter Hickman were added to the growing list of crashers, the latter's incident bringing out the Safety Car, with three laps added to the race for its period of intervention. During those crucial laps, Brookes snatched the final podium position from Kiyonari as he closed in on second placed Byrne, but it was too little too late for the Aussie. Jason O'Halloran took fourth ahead of Stuart Easton and Howie Mainwaring Smart.

Ellison employed the same tactics in race two, charging into the lead again with Kiyonari in hot pursuit from Byrne, Brookes and the Tyco BMW in the hands of Bridewell. Byrne, keen to set the record straight on his home track, displaced Kiyonari and then set about closing down on the runaway leader Ellison. Kiyonari, meanwhile, strayed off line and Brookes was through into third. Danny Johnson's heavy crash brought the Safety Car out and bunched the pack up, but Ellison was able to control things as racing resumed.

Byrne tried everything he knew to catch Ellison and although he closed to within a third of a second of him, there was no denying Ellison his first ever double. Brookes held solid in third ahead of Kiyonari, Easton, Bridewell and Mainwaring Smart. Danny Buchan ran eighth ahead of Billy McConnell and Jason O'Halloran whose Honda team-mate Dan Linfoot had been sidelined with a broken wrist after crashing in first free practice.

RACE 1 (33 LAPS)

1	ELLISON	JG Speedfit Kawasaki
2	BYRNE	PBM Kawasaki
3	BROOKES	Milwaukee Yamaha

RACE 2 (25 LAPS)

1	ELLISON	JG Speedfit Kawasaki
2	BYRNE	PBM Kawasaki
3	BROOKES	Milwaukee Yamaha

BSB CHAMPIONSHIP POINTS

			PP
1	BYRNE	85	14
2	ELLISON	79	15
3	BROOKES	58	3
4	EASTON	42	1
5	LINFOOT	33	3
6	BRIDEWELL / KIYONARI	28	0

MASERATI

GHIBLI

THE HEAD SAYS YES.
THE HEART SAYS DEFINITELY, YES.

MASERATI GHIBLI. THE ABSOLUTE OPPOSITE OF ORDINARY. *STARTING FROM £49,160*

THE NEW MASERATI GHIBLI IS POWERED BY A RANGE OF ADVANCED 3.0 LITRE V6 ENGINES WITH 8-SPEED ZF AUTOMATIC TRANSMISSION, INCLUDING, FOR THE FIRST TIME, A V6 TURBODIESEL ENGINE.

FOR MORE INFORMATION ON THE MASERATI GHIBLI, CALL 01943 871660 OR VISIT MASERATI.CO.UK

Official fuel consumption figures for Maserati Ghibli range in mpg (l/100km): Urban 18.0 (15.7) – 37.2 (7.6), Extra Urban 38.7 (7.3) – 56.5 (5.0), Combined 27.2 (10.4) – 47.9 (5.9). CO_2 emissions 242 – 158 g/km. Fuel consumption and CO_2 figures are based on standard EU tests for comparative purposes and may not reflect real driving results. Model shown is a Maserati Ghibli S at £69,638 On The Road including optional pearlescent paint at £1,776, 21" Titano design alloy wheels at £3,670 and Red brake callipers at £432.

www.maserati.co.uk

03
Oulton Park
02 - 04 May 2015

Top left: Brookes heads Bridewell, Byrne and indeed the rest of the pack through Cascades

Above: Martin Jessopp in action on the Riders BMW

Right: 'The Stalker' may have been in the paddock for longer than most but he still pushes hard

Below: Stuart Easton gets his trademark lightning start into Old Hall Corner

Top left: The slightest of errors saw Kiyo and Byrne crash out

Top right: Byrne gets a lift back to the pits from PBM team-mate, Easton

Bottom left: Kiyonari and Byrne have spent a lot of time racing at close quarters and, at this early part of the season, it appeared that 2015 was to be no different

Bottom right: Easton heads Ellison and Brookes

Left: Richard Cooper was having a strong outing on the Anvil Hire TAG Racing Kawasaki, as was Tommy Bridewell on the Tyco BMW (Bottom right)

Below: Parkes and Kennedy had a coming together at Hizzys

Above & top right: Brookes' request for an Apple watch may have been misinterpreted as race director Stuart Higgs hands over his Royal London pole position award

Oulton Park

VICTORIES FOR BRIDEWELL AND EASTON

James Ellison was not able to maintain his winning spree at his home track but the JG Speedfit Kawasaki rider left the Cheshire circuit with the lead in the title stakes after a third round of drama and incident as he packed the points on a day when others missed out.

The weekend posted a milestone for Milwaukee Yamaha, as for the first time their all-new R1 was powered onto pole position by Aussie Josh Brookes but that was to prove a false dawn when it came to the actual races as their former rider Tommy Bridewell took his, and Tyco BMW's, first victory of the season.

The Wiltshire rider led race one throughout, though he was hounded all of the way by Brookes, who took some consolation by bettering his own year-old lap record while Shane Byrne ran a close third, despite a scary moment at Clay Hill when his PBM Kawasaki snaked out of line at two thirds distance. His team-mate Stuart Easton ran fourth ahead of Buildbase BMW's Ryuichi Kiyonari with Ellison completing the top six.

Kiyonari capitalised on a poor start from Brookes to take the initiative in the second race with Byrne playing a determined game of catch-up, smashing the lap record as he closed in, but Bridewell passed him and then snatched the lead on the third lap, only to tip off shortly afterwards at Hizzy's.

Byrne attacked Kiyonari and by half distance they were trading places at the front of the pack, then Easton joined the fun, briefly grabbing second from Byrne but the defending champion re-grouped, took the Scot and then nosed into the lead. Kiyonari fought back and closed in, too close in fact, as he clipped Byrne at Hizzy's and both went down. Kiyo landed awkwardly and rebroke the same collarbone which had cost him his shot at last year's title.

Easton took the race victory, his first win in five years in the series, with Ellison following him home as Brookes completed the podium ahead of Michael Laverty having his best result of the season so far. The Ulsterman took fourth on the Tyco BMW ahead of Honda's Jason O'Halloran and Howie Mainwaring Smart on the Quattro Plant Bournemouth Kawasaki.

RACE 1	(18 LAPS)	
1	BRIDEWELL	Tyco BMW Motorrad
2	BROOKES	Milwaukee Yamaha
3	BYRNE	PBM Kawasaki

RACE 2	(18 LAPS)	
1	EASTON	PBM Kawasaki
2	ELLISON	JG Speedfit Kawasaki
3	BROOKES	Milwaukee Yamaha

	BSB CHAMPIONSHIP POINTS		PP
1	ELLISON	109	18
2	BYRNE	101	15
3	BROOKES	94	7
4	EASTON	80	6
5	BRIDEWELL	53	5
6	O'HALLORAN	42	0

Proud to be
part of the
PBM team

In our second year of backing the Paul Bird Motorsport team,
we enjoyed the highs and lows which makes BSB such an
enthralling series.

From the double 1-2 at Knockhill to the double crash at
Brands, it's been a truly memorable season. Once again for
Hager and our customers, it's been a privilege to be part of
the PBM team.

Snetterton 300

19 - 21 June 2015

Above: Linfoot leads Easton and Walker

Right: Brookes and O'Halloran wait to be called to the podium

Top right: Byrne gets the jump on O'Halloran

Below: The MCE British Superbike pack head towards the 'scary tree'

Left: O'Halloran was running his Honda at the front where it should be

Bottom left: Britain's fastest female motorcycle racer, Jenny Tinmouth, puts hers where it shouldn't be – upside down!

Below: Kiyo gets a Yamaha taxi back to the pits

Bottom: Broc Parkes leads the mid-pack through Riches

Top left: Jason O'Halloran was beginning to show his and the Honda's potential - here he leads James Ellison on the JG Speedfit Kawasaki

Top right: It is always going to be tight into Montreal as Easton, Bridewell, Ellison, Brookes et al fight for the same narrow strip of tarmac

Left: Reigning champion Shane 'Shakey' Byrne has enjoyed significant success at the Norfolk circuit. Again, he didn't disappoint

Above: Howie Mainwaring Smart took a tumble at Murrays

BYRNE FIRES BACK WITH DOUBLE WIN

If there was any pressure on him to deliver the goods, it hardly showed as Shane Byrne fired a double warning to his rivals that he was back in business, though it was not all as straightforward as it might have appeared.

In the opening race the PBM Kawasaki rider had to contend with an electronics issue that was affecting the quick shifter, but Byrne rode through it, took the win, his team solved the problem and next time out, it was all systems go and he used the power of the bike to the full.

That came after a dramatic qualifying session in which the weather intervened to a degree and several riders, among them Dan Linfoot, Victor Cox, Jakub Smrz and the series leading James Ellison all crashed, the latter sustaining damage to his JG Speedfit Kawasaki as well as a couple of broken ribs. Byrne, keeping a careful eye on his rivals and the fast improving conditions, saved the best for last to snatch pole away from Honda's Jason O'Halloran.

Byrne was swiftly away in the opening race, pursued by the twin Aussie threat of O'Halloran and Milwaukee Yamaha's Josh Brookes who was quickly on the attack despite a second row start, though he had to wait until three quarters distance to take over in second place ahead of his compatriot. By then Byrne was well in the clear and there was no catching him. Tommy Bridewell came in fourth, some cheer for Tyco BMW whose other rider Michael Laverty had been forced out, as had the luckless Ellison, due to a stretched chain.

Incidents early on in the second race saw Ryuichi Kiyonari, having another miserable time, overshoot the chicane, then tumble from his Buildbase BMW while Taylor Mackenzie had to jump clear as his WD-40 Kawasaki burst into flames as he powered into Oggies. Byrne was not distracted; he had full concentration as he led throughout with Brookes keeping him honest while O'Halloran ran third.

Byrne dominated, taking the victory by almost five seconds ahead of Brookes who hit back in the closing stages to take second from O'Halloran who was having his and Honda's best day of the season to that point. Laverty claimed fourth, ahead of Bridewell, Easton and Ellison, who finally rescued something from a tough weekend in Norfolk.

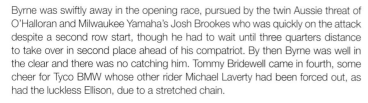

RACE 1	(16 LAPS)	
1	BYRNE	PBM Kawasaki
2	BROOKES	Milwaukee Yamaha
3	O'HALLORAN	Honda Racing

RACE 2	(16 LAPS)	
1	BYRNE	PBM Kawasaki
2	BROOKES	Milwaukee Yamaha
3	O'HALLORAN	Honda Racing

BSB CHAMPIONSHIP POINTS			PP
1	BYRNE	151	25
2	BROOKES	134	13
3	ELLISON	118	18
4	EASTON	99	6
5	BRIDEWELL	77	5
6	O'HALLORAN	74	2

Thank you for a great season

To all of our co-sponsors, team members and customers a huge thank you for what was a good first season with BMW Motorrad in 2015. With all the progress we have made we are all looking forward to what will be a fantastic 2016.

Knockhill

03 - 05 JULY 2015

Top left: Ellison, Laverty and Buchan line up on the grid

Centre: Although Brookes is an intense racer, he does have a light side

Top right: Laverty leads Byrne, Easton and Brookes out of the Hairpin

Bottom left: Further down the field, a close battle emerges between Lee Jackson on the Buildbase BMW, Howie Mainwaring Smart and Billy McConnell

Bottom right: Laverty and Easton at the Hairpin

Left: Brookes pushes hard over the Start/Finish

Above: Byrne on the limit once again as he squeezes under Easton

Right: Westmoreland leads Jackson, Kiyonari, McConnell and Iddon

Bottom left: Josh Waters on the Bennetts Suzuki

Bottom right: Byrne, Easton and Brookes at close quarters

Left: Fast-starting Easton leads into Scotsman on lap one

Bottom left: The leaders fight at the front of the field

Above: Another celebration wheelie from Shakey Byrne

Below: How a rider can pick out his pit board (never mind absorb the information on it) at 150mph is astonishing

Knockhill

BYRNE AND EASTON IN HISTORIC DOUBLE ONE-TWO

Shane Byrne made his intentions plain in qualifying as he powered in his second pole position in as many rounds, but it was not all plain sailing for the PBM Kawasaki rider, who moments after bettering the lap record to head off the threat of both his team-mate Stuart Easton and Josh Brookes by a split second, was tumbling into the gravel.

No harm was done as others began their race day on a downer with both Broc Parkes and Dan Linfoot sliding off in the morning warm-up though they made the race without too many problems. As race one got underway, it was Easton, aiming to become the first Scot since his mentor, the late Steve Hislop way back in 2002 to win a Superbike race on home soil, who made a brilliant start. But Byrne was there to spoil the party and he eased ahead at the Hairpin, and then led all of the way to the flag.

It was proving to be a race of attrition with a dozen riders, mostly through crashes, not making the finish which came amid some controversy as Michael Laverty came through from fourth in the closing five laps to take second on the road on the Tyco BMW ahead of both Easton and Milwaukee Yamaha's Brookes. After reviewing evidence of the action, it was deemed that Laverty gained an unfair advantage under yellow flags after James Rose had crashed, subsequently being penalised and classified in fourth.

Laverty was fast away at the start of the second race with James Ellison, eager to make up lost ground after his earlier crash, tucked in behind but ahead of Easton, Byrne and Brookes. Ellison made a mistake and dropped well back, and Byrne attacked Easton to run second and then at what should have been half-distance, taking the lead at the Hairpin. But within three laps the rains that had delayed the start of the action on Saturday returned, albeit only lightly, but it was enough to bring out the red flags.

Byrne, the leader at the time of the stoppage, led from pole in the restart and was never headed in the 11 lap sprint as he claimed maximum points for the fifth time in the campaign, half a second up on Easton who had to settle for second place again and an historic double one-two for Paul Bird's team. Brookes claimed third from the revitalised Ryuichi Kiyonari on the Buildbase BMW, Honda's Jason O'Halloran and Laverty.

For Ellison, who had braved the pain of a rib broken in the previous round, it was a pointless day as he pulled his JG Speedfit Kawasaki off to retire with a technical problem, though his closest rival in the Showdown stakes, Tommy Bridewell, fared little better, with only a seventh place in the opening race to show for his efforts on the Tyco BMW.

RACE 1	(30 LAPS)	
1	BYRNE	PBM Kawasaki
2	EASTON	PBM Kawasaki
3	BROOKES	Milwaukee Yamaha

RACE 2	(11 LAPS)	
1	BYRNE	PBM Kawasaki
2	EASTON	PBM Kawasaki
3	BROOKES	Milwaukee Yamaha

BSB CHAMPIONSHIP POINTS			PP
1	BYRNE	201	35
2	BROOKES	166	15
3	EASTON	139	12
4	ELLISON	118	18
5	O'HALLORAN	96	2
6	BRIDEWELL	86	5

DEFINITIVE CORPORATE AND PRIVATE CURRENCY EXCHANGE.

Expertise. Speed. Power.

Find out how
we can help you.

Phone
020 8712 8963

Email
info@globalreach-partners.com

Website
globalreach-partners.com

currency is our world

06

Brands Hatch GP

17 - 19 JULY 2015

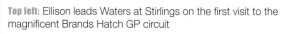

Top left: Ellison leads Waters at Stirlings on the first visit to the magnificent Brands Hatch GP circuit

Left: A packed crowd watch the start

Centre: Chris Walker suffered an engine failure but managed to leave the circuit at the earliest opportunity

Top right: Brookes leads Cooper, Ellison and Bridewell out of Strlings

Right: Byrne heads them all prior to his crash

Top left: Line astern action from Westmoreland, Parkes and Jackson as they leave lines whilst taking different lines

Bottom left: A full house to watch MCE BSB action at Paddock Hill

Above: The Tyco BMWs of Michael Laverty and Tommy Bridewell do battle under the watchful eye of John Hopkins and Luke Mossey

Below: Dan Linfoot runs his Honda on the racing line as Kiyonari cuts in tight on the run from Paddock Hill to Druids

Top left: Hopkins, Mossey and Iddon do battle

Top right: Brookes heads the field as he begins to realise the potential of the Milwaukee Yamaha

Bottom right: Richard Cooper put in a strong performance

Below & bottom left: Brookes can't hide his delight as he takes a full house, two race wins and the magnificent Monster Energy King of Brands trophy

BROOKES AT THE DOUBLE

Josh Brookes and the Milwaukee Yamaha team finally had their determined and hard work developing the all-new R1 road bike into a race winner rewarded with double success to underline their challenge for the crown on an afternoon of high drama and incident.

As a prelude to it all, qualifying had been sensational with first Brookes bettering the lap record, then local hero Shakey Byrne going even faster. Brookes hit back and came within 0.001secs of denying the PBM Kawasaki rider the pole position as the battle lines had been drawn.

Byrne was fast away in race one with Brookes in hot pursuit, followed by Richard Cooper on the Anvil Hire TAG Kawasaki, James Ellison on the JG Speedfit Kawasaki and Stuart Easton on the second PBM bike. They were all clear of Druids as Jason O'Halloran, Danny Buchan and Peter Hickman went down on an opening lap in which James Rose also fell.

Brookes took Byrne on the fourth lap and not long afterwards, the Safety Car was deployed as marshals dealt with the 155mph crash at Hawthorn of Stuart Easton who had impacted the barriers at high speed. Michael Rutter had also gone down at Westfield and then in something of a crash-fest, Martin Jessopp high-sided out also.

Brookes was looking solid, but Byrne was in hot pursuit and after setting his fastest lap, he too went down in similar fashion to his team-mate Easton, at the exact same corner. Cooper was second, and on the tail of Brookes and pushing the Aussie hard with Ellison third from the Tyco BMW duo of Tommy Bridewell and Michael Laverty. John Hopkins, returning to the series aboard the Lloyds British Moto Rapido Ducati in place of the injured Jakub Smrz, completed the top six.

Easton was ruled out of the second race with leg and ankle injuries and that enabled the full PBM crew to work on repairing Byrne's bike and he repaid their efforts by taking the lead, despite the battering he had endured. Brookes reeled him in and took the lead on the eighth lap at Druids and then eased to a memorable second victory of the day. Byrne headed off the close attentions of Cooper, who enjoyed his best ever day in MCE BSB as he finished third ahead of Ellison, Laverty and Billy McConnell aboard the Smiths BMW.

But as the attention began to focus on the Showdown, both Bridewell and Dan Linfoot tumbled in the second race, while the woes for former three-times champion Ryuichi Kiyonari continued with another pointless afternoon for the Buildbase BMW rider.

RACE 1	(20 LAPS)
1 BROOKES	*Milwaukee Yamaha*
2 COOPER	*Anvil Hire TAG Racing Kawasaki*
3 ELLISON	*JG Speedfit Kawasaki*

RACE 2	(20 LAPS)
1 BROOKES	*Milwaukee Yamaha*
2 BYRNE	*PBM Kawasaki*
3 COOPER	*Anvil Hire TAG Racing Kawasaki*

BSB CHAMPIONSHIP POINTS		PP
1 BYRNE	221	38
2 BROOKES	216	25
3 ELLISON	147	19
4 EASTON	139	12
5 O'HALLORAN	103	2
6 BRIDEWELL	99	5

Leading the way in
Motorcycle Accident
Management

MᶜAMS

Proud to support JG Speedfit
Kawasaki and James Ellison

Call 0845 054 1000
www.mc-ams.co.uk

139 NEW COURT WAY, ORMSKIRK, LANCASHIRE L39 2YT

dealernews
INDUSTRY
AWARDS
2015

RATED 9.7/10 ON
TRUSTPILOT

07
Thruxton
31 JULY - 02 AUGUST 2015

Top left: Martin Jessopp enjoys his outings at the fast Thruxton circuit

Top right: Byrne chases Linfoot through the Club Chicane

Above: TT legend Ian Hutchinson was deputising for the injured Stuart Easton

Left: Jason O'Halloran gets a message of support from his team-mate Dan Linfoot

Right: Brookes looking comfortable into the Club Chicane

GET WELL SOON JASON

Left: Brookes is smooth through the Club Chicane and totally oblivious to the chaos unfolding behind him as John Hopkins loses the front of his Moto Rapido Ducati (sequence below)

Top right: James Westmoreland showed some form in race one, putting his JG Speedfit Kawasaki on the podium

Bottom left: Michael Laverty flat out in the Hampshire countryside

Bottom centre: Three time BSB champion Kiyo had another difficult weekend

Bottom right: The fast Thruxton circuit can take its toll on man and machinery as Billy McConnell found out on the Smiths BMW

Top: A packed crowd enjoy the sunshine and the racing at the Complex

Centre sequence: The only mistake Josh Brookes made all weekend was the rather embarrassing slip off during his celebratory burn-out

Left: Luke Mossey is bound to be one to watch for the future as here he leads reigning champion Shane Byrne and Tommy Bridewell

Right: Good mates away from the track, Tommy Bridewell and Martin Jessopp celebrate with a joint burn-out on it

Thruxton

BROOKES ON TOP AS BYRNE STRUGGLES

Josh Brookes continued his love affair with the high-speed Hampshire circuit with a second winning double in as many rounds. The Aussie has a great pedigree, having enjoyed his first MCE BSB victory there five years earlier and last year powering to another double.

This time around, it was a continuation of that form. Full of confidence from his successes at Brands Hatch, Brookes bettered the lap record to take his second pole of the campaign; he led throughout both races and broke the nine-year-old lap record to take the lead in the standings. The only blemish on a perfect day for the Milwaukee Yamaha rider was the celebratory burn-out spoiled as the bike tipped him off, but with nothing more than dented pride.

In contrast to the fine form of Brookes, his arch-rival Shane Byrne was having a testing weekend on a circuit where he has struggled in the past. His three worst qualifying performances have been at Thruxton and this one left his PBM Kawasaki, lacking grip and handling, starting from the sixth row of the grid as he was just 17th fastest, though he was elevated one place by the enforced absence of Honda's Jason O'Halloran who sustained a badly broken leg in a high speed qualifying crash.

Brookes led from the start of the opener which was red-flagged after five laps as Christian Iddon and James Ellison crashed at Church on oil sprayed moments earlier as Richard Cooper's Anvil Hire TAG Kawasaki blew. The luckless Ellison suffered a broken wrist in the melee.

At the time, Byrne was running back in 13th, but the re-start gave him something of a lifeline and the chance to make up further ground. Out front Brookes was in charge, but John Hopkins was looking strong on the Lloyds British Moto Rapido Ducati until he was sidelined by a broken exhaust. Honda's Dan Linfoot took over in second place, ahead of James Westmoreland, who ended up taking his first MCE BSB podium on the JG Speedfit Kawasaki with Byrne's damage limitation ride taking him to fourth.

Next time out it was a similar story. Brookes charged ahead from the off, smashed the lap record on his second lap and pulled a comfortable lead over Hopkins. Linfoot got the better of Byrne, who was also under pressure from Howie Mainwaring Smart while Jack Kennedy and Christian Iddon were on the fringes of that slipstreaming pack.

Kennedy was looking good on the WD-40 Kawasaki, only to crash out of fifth at Campbell's, bringing out the Safety Car to the dismay of Brookes whose lead was eroded, though after that intervention he quickly roared back into the clear to take his fourth victory on the bounce.

Byrne scrapped hard to take second place from Luke Mossey, for whom third place on the Quattro Plant Kawasaki was his best MCE BSB result, making him the tenth rider so far this term to take a podium finish. Tommy Bridewell, a crasher in the first race after tangling with Danny Buchan, took fourth with his Tyco BMW team-mate Michael Laverty sixth and with Dan Linfoot sandwiched between them in fifth.

BSB CHAMPIONSHIP POINTS			PP
1	BROOKES	266	35
2	BYRNE	254	41
3	ELLISON	147	19
4	EASTON	139	12
5	LAVERTY	115	0
6	BRIDEWELL	112	5

RACE 1 (15 LAPS)	
1 BROOKES	Milwaukee Yamaha
2 LINFOOT	Honda Racing
3 WESTMORELAND	JG Speedfit Kawasaki

RACE 2 (20 LAPS)	
1 BROOKES	Milwaukee Yamaha
2 BYRNE	PBM Kawasaki
3 MOSSEY	Quattro Plant Tec-care Kawasaki

08
Cadwell Park
21 - 23 AUGUST 2015

Left: Once again, a packed crowed filled Cadwell (moved from its traditional bank holiday slot due to a clash with MotoGP) to witness the very best in British racing

Above: Amiable Swede, Filip Backlund, was back in the BSB paddock riding the Anvil Hire TAG Racing Kawasaki

Bottom left: Billy McConnell was getting to grips with the Smiths Racing BMW and put it on the race one podium

Below: Josh Brookes was once again on top form and on his way to two more victories

Top left: Jenny Tinmouth on board the Louth-based Honda Racing Fireblade

Left: Shaun Winfield was on the second of the Anvil Hire TAG Racing Kawasakis

Above: Josh Waters had another troubled outing on the Bennetts Suzuki

Bottom left: Peter Hickman always goes well at his local circuit - this year on the RAF Reserves BMW in the small but neatly run team of Lee Hardy

Bottom right: Brookes continued to thrill the crowds with his exploits over the famous Mountain and it was here, on the Cadwell podium that he felt the crowd really started to connect with him

Right: Dan Linfoot leads Josh Brookes and Lee Jackson through Hall Bends at arguably the most picturesque circuit on the calendar

Below: John Hopkins and Howie Mainwaring Smart had a coming together

Bottom left: Richard Cooper was drafted into the Buildbase BMW squad having parted with his former team

Bottom right: Christian Iddon leads Dan Linfoot through Barn Corner

Cadwell Park

BROOKES REMAINS UNSTOPPABLE

This was another perfect day for Josh Brookes as his domination continued unabated. He took a pole start for the opening race having shattered the eight-year-old lap record during qualifying and he used that to good effect, charging clear of the pursuing pack to plant his Milwaukee Yamaha a quarter of a second up by the end of the opening lap.

That lead swelled tenfold by the time the Safety Car came out as marshals dealt with the heavy crash of Danny Buchan at the Mountain but that proved little more than a hindrance as the Aussie upped the tempo, bettering the lap record as he was never headed, winning by almost two seconds.

Next time out, apart from no Safety Car, it was an action replay from Brookes as he won with ease, later apologising to the spectators for what he considered had been a boring race. It was all plain sailing for the Aussie as he extended his lead in the overall standings and for the first time moved ahead of Shane Byrne in the Podium Credit scores.

Defending champion Byrne was having another tough time, way off the pace on his PBM Kawasaki in qualifying as he and the team stripped the bike down as they considered if any issue from his big crash at Brands Hatch might have been left undiscovered. Byrne fought hard with two damage limitation rides into sixth and fourth places, but added no Podium Credits to his score.

Peter Hickman made local knowledge count again on the RAF Reserves BMW. In the corresponding round of last year, the Louth rider had taken his maiden victory in the series; this time around he was second in each of the races. Tommy Bridewell, who like Hickman had enjoyed his first MCE BSB race win at the circuit last term, was narrowly beaten in the scrap for third by Aussie Billy McConnell, taking his and the Smiths BMW team's first podium finish in the first race but the Tyco BMW rider hit back to take third next time out.

With Easton and Ellison on the sick list, Cadwell did not go any further to resolving who would join Brookes and Byrne in being qualified for the Showdown though it gave the opportunity for various riders. Amongst them was Luke Mossey on the Quattro Plant Kawasaki and Richard Cooper, who had switched teams to ride for Buildbase BMW, not forgetting Buchan, riding in Be Wiser Kawasaki colours. Sadly for the old guard of Chris Walker and Ryuichi Kiyonari, their seasons were fizzling out.

RACE 1 (18 LAPS)	
1 BROOKES	Milwaukee Yamaha
2 HICKMAN	RAF Reserves BMW
3 McCONNELL	Smiths Racing BMW

RACE 2 (18 LAPS)	
1 BROOKES	Milwaukee Yamaha
2 HICKMAN	RAF Reserves BMW
3 BRIDEWELL	Tyco BMW Motorrad

BSB CHAMPIONSHIP POINTS		PP
1 BROOKES	316	45
2 BYRNE	277	41
3 ELLISON	147	19
4 BRIDEWELL	141	6
5 EASTON	139	12
6 LAVERTY	126	0

READY TO RACE
»www.ktm.com

www.kiska.com

Photos: R. Schedl, H. Mitterbauer

The illustrated vehicles may vary in selected details from the production models and some illustrations feature optional equipment available at additional cost.

RC390

PURE RACING

Hyper-agile, fast and extremely sporty. Apply power and manoeuvrability
to the tarmac every day — whether it be on the road or with your knee to
the ground on the racetrack. High-tech premium parts, perfectly finished and
optimally coordinated with each other. Uncompromisingly READY TO RACE.

» Water-cooled 373.2 cc DOHC engine
» 44 hp (32 kW) of power / 35 Nm max. torque
» Best power-to-weight ratio in it's class
» Aerodynamically optimum fairing
» Racing geometry

INCLUDING STANDARD ABS

A2 Suitable for A2 driving licence!

 /UKKTM   @KTM_UK   KTM_UK

09 Oulton Park

04 - 06 September 2015

Below: Danny 'Boom Boom' Buchan celebrates his best result of the season

Right: Shane Byrne leads the field in front of yet another packed BSB crowd

Bottom left: A mechanical issue during his warm up lap in qualifying saw Josh Brookes start from the back of the race one grid

Bottom right: 'Old but Gold' Chris Walker celebrated his 300th British Superbike race start

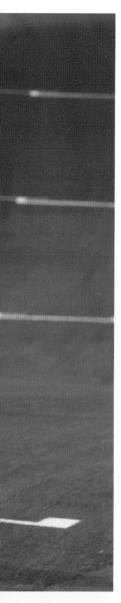

Top left: James Ellison took the JG Speedfit Kawasaki to second in race one

Bottom left: Dan Linfoot on the Honda Racing Fireblade

Above: Brookes and Byrne at close quarters

Below: Brookes, Byrne and Bridewell

Top left: Shakey has a foot off the peg moment as he tries desperately to keep the lead from a charging Josh Brookes

Bottom left: Buchan chases Ellison through Lodge

Left: Michael Laverty asking a lot of his front Pirelli - still on the brake and over the white line

Above: Howie Mainwaring Smart ended up on the wrong side of the Armco

Below: Brookes appears to have Shakey as a pillion as they battle over the Start/Finish line ahead of Linfoot and Ellison

Oulton Park

BYRNE FIGHTS BACK BUT BROOKES STAYS ON TOP

The theoretical scriptwriters for the Showdown could hardly have come up with this dramatic and enthralling confrontation between the top two in the standings as the title race took another twist.

Josh Brookes and Shane Byrne both overcame engine problems in the triple-header round to take the top step of the podium, Byrne twice to Brookes' once, and after the third race of the weekend the Aussie had the edge but now by just two points.

The problems for Brookes began on his out lap in qualifying, forcing him to return to the Milwaukee Yamaha pit with a mechanical problem which necessitated an engine change. The team swapped not one, but two engines to allow him to take his place on the back of the grid for the Saturday afternoon race. In contrast Byrne and his PBM Kawasaki team had worked through the problems that had dogged the champion in the previous two rounds and he took pole, shattering the Cheshire circuit lap record in the process.

Byrne led race one throughout, finally matching his racing number with career victory number 67, as JG Speedfit Kawasaki's James Ellison, nursing that broken wrist, trailed him home, ensuring that he had joined Brookes and Byrne as a Title Fighter in the Showdown.

Danny Buchan took third, his best finish so far, on the Be Wiser Kawasaki, clear of Brookes who had carved through the pack to take fourth. Ironically the Aussie, never a lover of Safety Car intervention, moaned that maybe it should have been deployed when Christian Iddon crashed his Bennetts Suzuki at Island with four laps to go, bunching the pack to his advantage.

Brookes needed none of that next time out as he stormed into the lead, but he was being harassed all of the way by Byrne until the penultimate lap of the race when the challenge ended. Byrne suddenly slowed and pulled off, a blown engine had ended his hopes of repeating his race one victory. Brookes took an easy win ahead of Buchan, who had bettered his best in less than a day. Honda's Dan Linfoot took third ahead of Luke Mossey, Ellison and Peter Hickman.

Flying Scot Stuart Easton, whose comeback from the broken leg sustained at Brands Hatch had ended with another heavy crash at Cascades in qualifying, could only watch as his hopes of qualifying into the Showdown ended in the final race of the day as Linfoot and Tyco BMW's Michael Laverty scored the points needed to go ahead of him.

The race saw Brookes charge into the lead, pursued by Byrne and Bridewell, who was keen to make amends from the previous day's DNF and a crash earlier in the afternoon at Cascades. The Safety Car was deployed in this race after Shaun Winfield's heavy crash, and on the resumption Byrne tried a lunge for the lead, but lost a place to Bridewell. He fought back, finally taking the lead at Shell on the penultimate lap, and holding off Brookes to win with Bridewell third from Buchan, Ellison and Linfoot.

When the points were tallied up, it was Bridewell, Laverty and Linfoot who had done enough to secure their places in the Showdown alongside Brookes, Byrne and Ellison.

RACE 1	(18 LAPS)	
1	BYRNE	PBM Kawasaki
2	ELLISON	JG Speedfit Kawasaki
3	BUCHAN	Be Wiser Kawasaki

RACE 2	(18 LAPS)	
1	BROOKES	Milwaukee Yamaha
2	BUCHAN	Be Wiser Kawasaki
3	LINFOOT	Honda Racing

RACE 3	(18 LAPS)	
1	BYRNE	PBM Kawasaki
2	BROOKES	Milwaukee Yamaha
3	BRIDEWELL	Tyco BMW Motorrad

BSB CHAMPIONSHIP POINTS		
1	BROOKES	553
2	BYRNE	551
3	ELLISON	522
4	BRIDEWELL	507
5	LINFOOT	507
6	LAVERTY	500

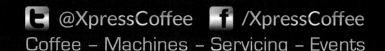

10 TT Circuit Assen

18 - 20 September 2015

Left: The leading pack charge into the opening corner of Haarbocht at the 'Cathedral of Speed'

Right: The look of concentration as Shakey prepares for the off

Bottom left: Jack Kennedy in aggressive mood through the Geert Timmer Chicane

Bottom right: Peter Hickman ahead of Buchan, Kennedy and McConnell

Top left: Another celebration wheelie from Brookes as he kicks off the Showdown in style

Top right: It's all getting a bit crowded as the Showdown begins

Left: Everyone wants to be safely through Strubben

Above: John Hopkins and Michael Laverty battle it out

Left: Linfoot made a tyre gamble in race two based on the ever present threat of rain, and extended a healthy lead only for the gamble to fail. He was subsequently caught and overhauled by the rest of the field before the end of the race

Bottom left: Lee Jackson was enjoying a strong season and is seen here leading Walker, Jessopp and Smrz

Above: Ellison held a strong advantage on a drying track but Brookes overhauled him to take the win

Below: Luke Mossey had another good showing in Holland, seen here with Byrne, Cooper and Iddon

BROOKES TAKES CHARGE AS BYRNE STRUGGLES

Josh Brookes was ready for the fight as the Showdown roared into action and the Milwaukee Yamaha rider scorched to his fourth pole start at record pace, although James Ellison, buoyed by signing a contract extension through to the end of the 2016 season challenged hard aboard his JG Speedfit Kawasaki, running only a third of a second down.

In contrast Shane Byrne was on the back foot, a full second down, fifth fastest on the PBM Kawasaki and with it all to do, Byrne found something for the first race and was able to run third, while Brookes grabbed the initiative and was never headed, bettering the lap record as he pulled well clear of Ellison who was always solid in second. Byrne, however, was under attack with Michael Laverty harassing him and with six laps to go, squeezed his Tyco BMW into third place at the defending champion's expense to take his first podium finish of the campaign.

John Hopkins took fifth on the Lloyds British Moto Rapido Ducati from Richard Cooper on the Buildbase BMW, Bennetts Suzuki rider Christian Iddon and Tommy Bridewell on the second Tyco BMW. Bridewell then compounded a bad day at the office by crashing out of the second race.

Then, as so often happens at this circuit, the rain showers rolled in, crucially one just as the riders began their warm-up lap for the second Superbike race. The start was delayed before another attempt to get the action underway was aborted and then, declared wet, though the track was drying fast, eventually the race got underway.

Most favoured running on slicks but one of the exceptions was Honda's Dan Linfoot, who opted for wets in a brave gamble to peg back points. He led for four laps, but then dropped back, finishing last as the track dried, and with it his title hopes all but gone. Brookes charged ahead, but then had a major scare as his bike snaked out of line. He held on to the R1 but lost four places as Luke Mossey led for a lap on his Quattro Plant Kawasaki before Ellison took over.

Behind them there was the gathering force of Brookes as he re-grouped and picked up places, making big inroads into the advantage held by Ellison and then swooping through into the lead with three laps remaining to complete his fourth winning double of the campaign, boosting his victory tally to nine. Byrne was back in fifth, losing more ground on Brookes and also coming under pressure to hold onto second place overall as Ellison enjoyed a rich points haul with a brace of seconds. Rookie Mossey matched his best result with third ahead of the determined Cooper while Iddon rounded off a strong day in sixth.

RACE 1	(18 LAPS)	
1	BROOKES	Milwaukee Yamaha
2	ELLISON	JG Speedfit Kawasaki
3	LAVERTY	Tyco BMW Motorrad

RACE 2	(18 LAPS)	
1	BROOKES	Milwaukee Yamaha
2	ELLISON	JG Speedfit Kawasaki
3	MOSSEY	Quattro Plant Tec-care Kawasaki

BSB CHAMPIONSHIP POINTS		
1	BROOKES	603
2	BYRNE	575
3	ELLISON	562
4	LAVERTY	523
5	BRIDEWELL	516
6	LINFOOT	509

JG Speedfit®

The Push-fit People

Speedfit Technology is built into the DNA of all our push-fit fittings. The distinctive appeal lies within its flexibility of application, high reliability of performance, longevity of service and suitability to a wide variety of industries.

The core technology behind a JG Speedfit plumbing fitting is the same concept incorporated in all John Guest fittings serving the needs of industries as diverse as drinks dispense, pneumatics, compressed air, water purification, drinks vending and telecommunications.

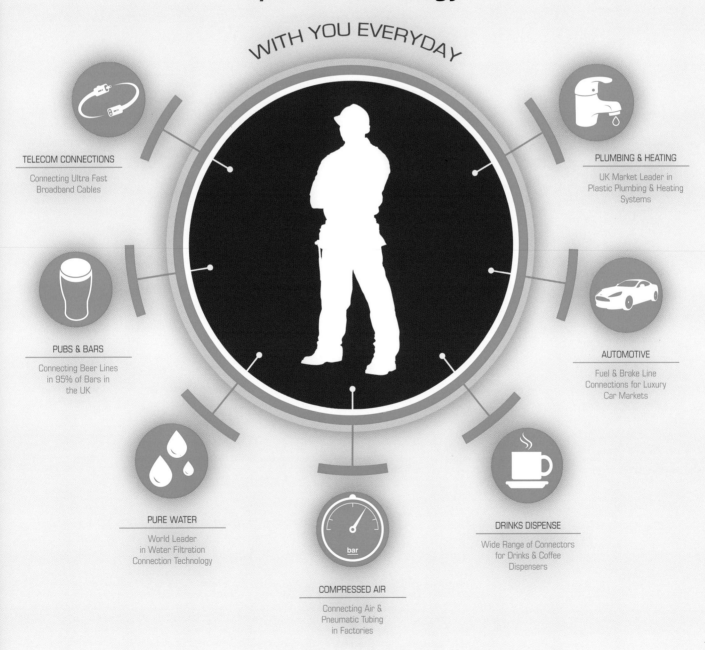

Speedfit® Technology

WITH YOU EVERYDAY

TELECOM CONNECTIONS
Connecting Ultra Fast
Broadband Cables

PLUMBING & HEATING
UK Market Leader in
Plastic Plumbing & Heating
Systems

PUBS & BARS
Connecting Beer Lines
in 95% of Bars in
the UK

AUTOMOTIVE
Fuel & Brake Line
Connections for Luxury
Car Markets

PURE WATER
World Leader
in Water Filtration
Connection Technology

DRINKS DISPENSE
Wide Range of Connectors
for Drinks & Coffee
Dispensers

COMPRESSED AIR
Connecting Air &
Pneumatic Tubing
in Factories

speedfit.co.uk

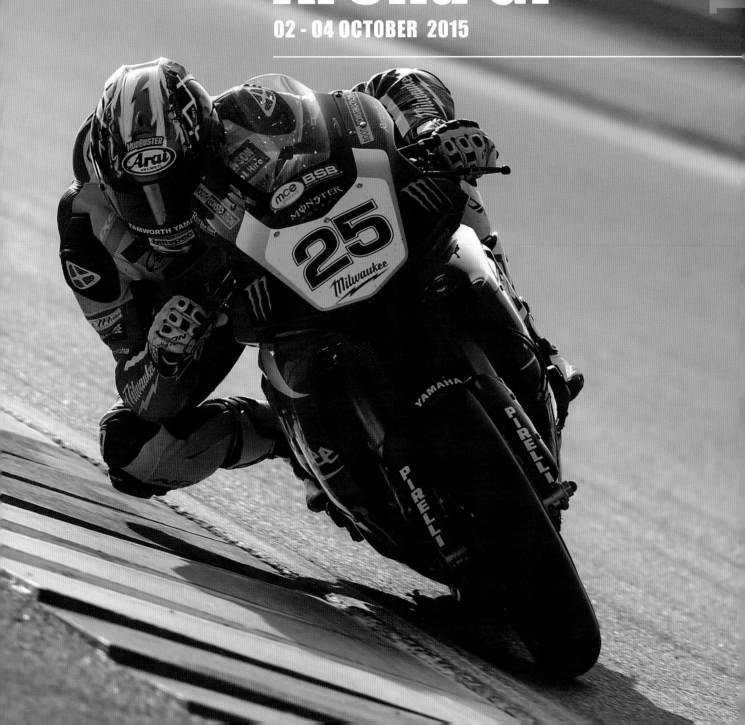

Silverstone Arena GP

02 - 04 OCTOBER 2015

Top left: Brookes and Ellison had a close battle in the early part of the race

Left & above: Peter Hickman had a solid ride only for his bike to catch fire on the slowing down lap leaving him to hitch a lift back to the pits

Top right: Brookes leads Hickman and Linfoot

Right: Hopkins, Bridewell, Cooper and McConnell exit Vale

Top: Everyone struggled for grip at Silverstone although looking at the commitment from James Ellison and Shakey Byrne, you wouldn't believe it

Left: Smrz, Mainwaring Smart and Stapleford. Stapleford had just wrapped up the Motorpoint Supersport title and with James Westmoreland parting ways with the JG Speedfit team Stapleford took his place

Above: Filip Backlund is chased by Jed Metcher on the Gearlink Kawasaki

Left: Byrne heads the pack through Vale while Brookes, aware that tyre life was a compromise, made a cautious start

Above: Mossey, Mainwaring Smart and Smrz

Bottom left: Last corner, last lap. Both Ellison and Byrne are desperate for drive as they get on the gas with full lock and smoke pouring from the tyres

Below: Brookes slots under Byrne

Silverstone Arena GP

BROOKES' DOMINATION CONTINUES

Josh Brookes continued his dominant form as the Milwaukee Yamaha rider left no doubt of his intent as he scorched to pole with a Superbike lap time that would have put him on the back row of the recent British MotoGP grid.

Then, despite anxieties shared with his rivals about tyre selection and grip issues for the two races, he duly completed his fifth winning double. These successes, however, had been hard earned with his fellow Title Fighters determined to maintain their already slim hopes of the crown, but try as they might, they eventually succumbed to the stylish Australian.

In the opening race, Brookes had made the break but the hard-charging James Ellison overhauled him at half distance, running his JG Speedfit Kawasaki at the head of the pack, while Shane Byrne, fresh from signing a one-year extension to his contract with Paul Bird's team, came through from a fourth row start to run second on the PBM Kawasaki.

Brookes was third with three laps remaining, but not for long, as he re-asserted himself, taking the victory by a little over half a second from Byrne while Ellison dropped back to an eventual fifth. Peter Hickman, always on the edge of the leaders, took third on the RAF Reserves BMW, but then stopped on the slow-down lap as his bike took fire, although the flames were soon extinguished. Of the other Title Fighters, Michael Laverty took sixth, just ahead of Dan Linfoot while Tommy Bridewell was ninth.

Byrne had pole position for the second race and while he led for the first lap, it was Ellison again who took up the front-running challenge with Honda Racing's Linfoot joining the action at the sharp end while Brookes, who was squeezed wide at the first corner, fought back from eighth on the first lap. Laverty on the Tyco BMW was also on the charge, but Brookes took the lead on lap 9, ahead of Linfoot and Laverty as Ellison's hopes faltered, the Cumbrian rider dropping out of contention, and the points with big grip problems.

Byrne too was struggling and slipped back to fifth, but out front Brookes surged clear, taking his eleventh victory by over three seconds from Laverty and Linfoot for whom the podium finishes were too little too late to keep them in the title chase. Christian Iddon took his best finish of fourth on the Bennetts Suzuki.

Luke Stapleford, who secured the Motorpoint British Supersport crown in the opening Silverstone race, made a positive debut in the top flight on the JG Speedfit Kawasaki team's second bike, scoring points in the second race while Danny Buchan, thrown a lifeline to race on after the demise of the Be Wiser Kawasaki team, bounced back from a first race tumble to score points next time out on the PBM Kawasaki as he deputised for the injured Stuart Easton.

In terms of the race for the title, Silverstone's results meant only one of two riders could win the crown leaving it to be determined from either Brookes, with a huge 47 point advantage, ahead of Byrne.

RACE 1	(18 LAPS)			BSB CHAMPIONSHIP POINTS	
1	BROOKES	Milwaukee Yamaha	1	BROOKES	653
2	BYRNE	PBM Be Wiser Kawasaki	2	BYRNE	606
3	HICKMAN	RAF Reserves BMW	3	ELLISON	573
			4	LAVERTY	553
RACE 2	(18 LAPS)		5	LINFOOT	534
1	BROOKES	Milwaukee Yamaha			
2	LAVERTY	Tyco BMW Motorrad	6	BRIDEWELL	531
3	LINFOOT	Honda Racing			

TAMWORTH YAMAHA

Tamworth's Exclusive Premier Yamaha Dealer

2015 MCN Awards
Dealer of the Year Central - Single Franchise

Tamworth Yamaha is a family-run business, passionate about ensuring that all of our customers enjoy a proactive experience in an environment where they can share their passion for bikes with others

We pride ourselves on carrying the most comprehensive range of new Yamaha motorcycles and scooters in the UK

We are also Yamaha's largest centre for genuine parts and accessories

We hold the largest demonstrator fleet in theUK, allowing the customer to experience the fantastic Yamaha range

Competition and Enduro machines are also part of our extensive portfolio

In summary - if it's Yamaha - it's Tamworth Yamaha. UK's leading Supersport specialist with R1, R3, R6 and R125

Jonathan and Lisa pride themselves on delivering the highest levels of customer satisfaction where nothing is too much trouble and where every customer is equally important as the next.

Proud sponsor of Josh Brookes - 2015 British Superbike Champion

Academy Workshop   Genuine Parts and Accessories   Apparel and Clothing Centre   Open 7 days

www.tamworthyamaha.com   info@tamworthyamaha.com

mce

12

Brands Hatch GP

16 - 18 OCTOBER 2015

THE SHOWDOWN

Above: Ellison, Laverty and Smrz head up to Druids

Right: Another packed Brands Hatch grid

Below: It's all charge as they prepare for the drop down Paddock Hill

Bottom right: Shakey was prepared to fight all the way for the Championship

Top left: Brookes was intent on taking his maiden title in style and took the fight to Byrne who this time had no answer

Left & below: Josh Brookes admires the Champion's helmet - another one for his already vast collection and celebrates his first MCE Insurance British Superbike Championship victory

Above: A happy Milwaukee Yamaha team

Top left: With Josh Brookes having wrapped up the championship, there were battles all through the field

Above: Brookes gets the jump from Byrne and Ellison

Below: The front-runners were swapping places with every lap

Left: Brookes is inch-perfect as he drives out of Stirlings, closely followed by Byrne

Above: Title wrapped up and still 'tinkering' although this time it was to get the bike ready for the celebration lap. Brookes had made his only mistake of the Showdown in the final race when unsighted, he clipped a kerb with his engine casing, the front folded and he slid off

Top right: Byrne still wanted to go out in style at what is considered his home circuit and having succumbed to Brookes' relentless pressure throughout the Showdown, Shakey's Paul Bird Motorsport team allowed Brookes to run the number one plate for the final two races

Brands Hatch GP

BROOKES CROWNED BEFORE THE FALL

Josh Brookes was keen to get the job done as yet again, the Milwaukee Yamaha rider dictated terms in qualifying with another scintillating pole position as light rain threatened. As it turned out, that set the momentum for the Aussie ahead of what was to be a near perfect weekend.

Defending champion Shane Byrne knew that he had to beat Brookes in Saturday's first of the three races to keep his own title hopes alive and the PBM Kawasaki rider rode as hard as he's ever done in what proved to be a vain attempt. Brookes led for a couple of laps, then Byrne went ahead as they traded places half a dozen times before just into the second half of the race, Brookes made the decisive move and then charged to victory. With it came the crown which he had been striving for in his seven year BSB tenure. Byrne finished second, gracious in defeat with the Moto Rapido Ducati of John Hopkins finally making it onto the podium.

Brookes joked that he would have a glass of champagne to celebrate, but not too much as "you can't rock up for two races with a hangover." Defeated, Byrne was eager to put one over the champion and that again provided an intense scrap for supremacy as the two giants of the series battled for glory in race two. They swapped positions at the head of the pack before Brookes made the telling move on lap seven, en route to victory number 13 of a campaign that had been turned around for him at the July meeting at the Kent circuit.

Expectations of Brookes taking an unprecedented seven straight wins in the Showdown sequence were high despite him running back in sixth place on the opening lap of the final race before making his way up to second in the early stages. But as he attacked Michael Laverty for the lead on the eighth lap, the unthinkable happened. Brookes clipped the kerb at the exit of Graham Hill Bend and crashed out in what was to be his only mistake and non-finish of the year.

Laverty had no problems and took his first victory of the campaign on the Tyco BMW ahead of James Ellison on the JG Speedfit Kawasaki who had taken second from Byrne on the penultimate lap. Byrne, with a pair of seconds and a third, was the series runner-up, something he vowed to rectify next year as he re-groups with Paul Bird's team that switches to Ducati. Ellison consolidated his third place as Christian Iddon, with two top finishes in the final round, underlined his potential on the Bennetts Suzuki.

FINAL CHAMPIONSHIP STANDINGS		
1	BROOKES	703
2	BYRNE	662
3	ELLISON	614
4	LAVERTY	601
5	LINFOOT	556
6	BRIDEWELL	545

RACE 1	(20 LAPS)	
1	BROOKES	Milwaukee Yamaha
2	BYRNE	PBM Be Wiser Kawasaki
3	HOPKINS	Moto Rapido Ducati

RACE 1	(19 LAPS)	
1	BROOKES	Milwaukee Yamaha
2	BYRNE	PBM Be Wiser Kawasaki
3	LAVERTY	Tyco BMW Motorrad

RACE 1	(20 LAPS)	
1	LAVERTY	Tyco BMW Motorrad
2	ELLISON	JG Speedfit Kawasaki
3	BYRNE	PBM Be Wiser Kawasaki

BRITISH SUPERBIKE CHAMPIONSHIP

WE R1

Developed without compromise using YZR-M1 MotoGP technology, the R1 was born for the track. 200PS, 179kg dry and 1,405mm wheelbase give an insight into its capabilities. . The all new crossplane engine, short wheelbase chassis and cutting edge design has created a new generation of Superbike, which, in the hands of Josh Brookes has smashed lap records and dominated the 2015 British Superbike Championship.

And Josh didn't even race with the high-tech electronics fitted to the standard R1. The central nervous system uses a 6-axis Inertial Measurement Unit that constantly senses chassis motion in 3D, creating controllability over traction, slides, front wheel lift, braking and launches. Imagine if Josh had this on his BSB bike. Yamaha R1. We R1.

www.yamaha-motor.eu/uk RAC YAMALUBE

 **YAMAHA**
Revs your Heart

Motorpoint British Supersport Championship

STAPLEFORD SUPREME

Unlike previous seasons, which saw the title go down to the wire, the 2015 Motorpoint British Supersport Championship was ultimately dominated by one rider – Luke Stapleford.

Coming into his fifth season in the class, the Profile Racing Triumph rider saw off the early challenge of Kyle Ryde to storm clear in the title standings and with a record number of wins totalling 14 during the course of the season, he ended the year with more points scored than anyone in the class ever before.

The Leicestershire rider signalled his intentions right from the first round when he took first and second at his local Donington Park and it set the tone for the remainder of the year. Indeed, such was his consistency, apart from three DNFs, the only time he didn't finish on the podium was in the second race at Knockhill when he was placed fourth.

Ryde's season fizzled out somewhat in the second half of the year, never finishing higher than fourth in the final eight races. However, the Derbyshire teenager had a strong season on the PacedayZ Trackdays Yamaha taking two wins and 13 podiums in total on his way to second overall. He also took a brilliant rostrum position as a wild card at the British round of the World Supersport Championship at Donington Park.

His lull towards the end of the season allowed Glenn Irwin (Gearlink Kawasaki) and Jake Dixon (Smiths Racing Triumph) the opportunity to close in and Dixon only missed out on second overall by just seven points. He started and ended the year strongly with his dip in form coming mid-season when a ten-race run saw him take only three podiums and fail to finish on four occasions.

It cost him dearly, but it was still a good year for the 19-year-old with Irwin also impressing throughout. His all-action style won him an army of new followers as he challenged for the race wins most weekends. With a strong year on the roads too, a new chapter beckons for the Northern Irishman in 2016 as he makes the move to British Superbikes with the PBM Ducati squad.

The other regular front-runners were the Team Traction Control Yamaha pairing of James Rispoli and Andrew Reid. American rider Rispoli got quicker as the year wore on and did everything but win a race whilst Reid's strong debut season was only ended by a broken wrist at Oulton Park in September.

Sam Hornsey, Ben Wilson and Luke Hedger also enjoyed solid seasons whilst the stand out performer in the Evo Championship was Joe Collier. Not only did he win the concurrently-run class by a commanding 142 points from Marshall Neill, he also finished tenth overall in the main championship.

CHAMPIONSHIP POSITIONS		
1	Luke STAPLEFORD	471
2	Kyle RYDE	344
3	Jake DIXON	337
4	Glenn IRWIN	320
5	James RISPOLI	256
6	Ben WILSON	185

Pirelli National Superstock 1000 Championship

HOUSE OF ELLIOTT

After a season-long struggle between Northern Ireland compatriots Josh Elliott and Alastair Seeley, it was Elliott who eventually came out on top with the 21-year-old putting together a remarkably consistent year.

The Morello Racing Kawasaki rider belied his age as he finished first or second in 11 of the 12 races, only a spill at Brands Hatch in July, when pressured into a mistake by Seeley, blotting his copybook. Five wins were taken in total and he was able to wrap up the title with a round to spare and a move to the premier British Superbike Championship now surely beckons.

Elder statesman Seeley, however, is a wily old competitor and he ensured Elliott had to work for the championship every inch of the way. A DNF at Knockhill hit the Tyco BMW rider's chances hard, but four wins kept him in the hunt and it was only when he got pushed off track whilst battling for the win at Silverstone that prevented the title going into the final round.

Class regular Hudson Kennaugh was a thorn in the side of Elliott and Seeley all year long and took three wins himself. Five podiums in the first five races made the fast-talking South African a serious title contender but two non scores mid-season saw him fall behind and he ultimately had to settle for third overall on the Trik-Moto/Bahnstormer BMW.

Another series regular, Luke Quigley, took fourth overall on the Formwise/Bathams BMW with no less than nine finishes inside the top six and with a podium at Silverstone, it was the perfect way for the Midlands rider to bow out of the sport after a long and successful career.

One place further back in the final standings was Adam Jenkinson, who had a mixed year for the Northern Escalator Installations team. Starting the year with the new R1 Yamaha, the Manchester rider finished on the podium at only the second round but a big crash at Donington Park saw him miss three further rounds. He bounced back towards the end of the year and, after switching to BMW, he was back on the podium at the final round.

Behind these five, there was a great battle for the remainder of the top ten leaderboard places with James East (Downshift Motorsport Kawasaki), Jesse Trayler (MSS Colchester Kawasaki), Michael Robertson (MRR Kawasaki) and Alex Olsen (Moto Breakers Kawasaki) all standing on the podium at various times. Dominic Usher (DU Racing BMW), Josh Wainwright (Connect Kawasaki) and James Egan (MWR Motorsports Ducati) also enjoyed a solid year.

	CHAMPIONSHIP POSITIONS	
1	Josh ELLIOTT	245
2	Alastair SEELEY	193
3	Hudson KENNAUGH	166
4	Luke QUIGLEY	127
5	Adam JENKINSON	104
6	James EAST	100

Pirelli National Superstock 600 Championship

Four wins in the opening four rounds laid the foundations for Mason Law's assault on the title and with two more victories added later in the year, he ran out a convincing winner of the series.

The NMT No Limits Kawasaki had shown glimpses of his potential in 2014 but this year saw a more confident and mature Law and he made it count. Those first four rounds gave him control of the title race and the second half of the season saw him do exactly what he needed to do at every round to rack up the points.

Indeed, he was only off the podium twice all year, but he was made to work very hard for his title by Ben Currie who was almost as consistent on the PacedayZ Trackdays Yamaha. He followed Law home in three of the first four rounds before taking his first victory of the year at Knockhill.

It allowed him to close the gap briefly to Law but a DNF at Cadwell and two fifth place finishes at Thruxton and Oulton Park respectively saw the Australian slip back.

Indeed, he almost missed out on second overall as Tarran Mackenzie (Stauff Connect Academy Kawasaki) put in a late surge to close to within three points. The younger of the Mackenzie clan was the fastest rider in the second half of the season, taking four wins, but three non finishes meant he was always playing catch up to Law and Currie.

These three were the dominant riders of the 2015 season with the remainder of the field squabbling over the lower leaderboard places and it was Andrew Irwin who sealed fourth overall when he took his third podium of the year with third place at the final round.

Joe Francis (Team Traction Control) looked like he had the position sewn up, but he moved up to the Supersport class for the last few rounds, replacing injured team-mate Andrew Reid. Tied on points, Francis lost out to Irwin due to the Northern Ireland rider's second place finish at Knockhill.

As always, a whole host of other riders got to stand on the podium in what was again one of the most fiercely contested classes. These included Jordan Weaving (NMT No Limits Kawasaki), Brad Jones (BJ Racing Yamaha), Dan Stamper (Allied Racing Kawasaki), Tom Ward (Go Racing Developments Yamaha) and Moto-Breakers Kawasaki team-mates Bradley Ray and Wayne Ryan all enjoying their moments of glory.

CHAMPIONSHIP POSITIONS		
1	Mason LAW	239
2	Ben CURRIE	180
3	Tarran MACKENZIE	177
4	Andrew IRWIN	103
5	Joe FRANCIS	103
6	Jordan WEAVING	78

DEROUE AND OWENS CLAIM HONOURS

An exciting season-long battle for the HEL Performance Motostar British Championship eventually went the way of Dutchman Scott Deroue and the Redline KTM team after he overhauled Taz Taylor in the final third of the season.

The former Moto3 Grand Prix rider arrived in the UK looking to rebuild his career and he did exactly that with a series of high class performances that saw him finish on the podium on no less than 20 occasions. With 12 wins and only one DNF, the pressure applied ultimately told on Taylor.

The RS Racing KTM rider led the way for the first half of the season and had the better of Deroue but with four non scores he fell behind his rival. He still took nine wins, however, and with the title having been lost at Silverstone, he switched to a 125cc machine for the final round of the year at Brands Hatch and promptly took a victory!

The duo were the class acts of the Moto 3-dominated field with Ed Rendell, last year's 125cc GP champion, the best of the rest. Switching to the Banks Racing Honda, Rendell wasn't able to take a win, such was the dominance of Deroue and Taylor, but he had the next highest tally of podiums with 12.

With Deroue and Taylor running away with matters at the head of the field, the battles for the final podium position were equally hard fought and were very much an international affair. Spain's Dani Saez (Repli Cast Moto3), the strong Dutch contingent of Jorel Boerboom (FPW Racing), Vasco van der Valk (ILR) and Mike Brouwers (Joma), Sweden's Alex Persson and Germany's Christoph Beinlich all had their moments, Saez and Boerboom particularly impressing.

Charlie Nesbitt (Repli Cast), Jake Archer (RS Racing), Elliot Lodge (Team Essential/SP125) and Georgina Polden (RS Racing) kept the UK flag flying whilst the only other race winner during the year was Bradley Ray, who took first and second at the opening round.

There was again a race within a race with the 125cc GP class again catered for although they were less competitive than in previous years as the Moto3 machines came into the ascendancy. It was Andrew Sawford who led in the early stages of the season, but Josh Owens soon got into his stride and 12 victories allowed him to romp clear, his eventual winning margin over Mark Clayton a whopping 165 points.

CHAMPIONSHIP POSITIONS - MOTO 3		
1	Scott DEROUE	473
2	Taz TAYLOR	354
3	Edward RENDELL	262
4	Dani SAEZ	228
5	Jorel BOERBOOM	222
6	Charlie NESBITT	174

CHAMPIONSHIP POSITIONS - 125CC GP		
1	Josh OWENS	435
2	Mark CLAYTON	270
3	Andrew SAWFORD	255
4	Liam DELVES	249
5	Wesley JONKER	246
6	Cameron HORSMAN	228

HEL Performance British Motostar Championship

Santander Consumer Finance
KTM British Junior Cup

STARS OF TOMORROW

The Santander Consumer Finance KTM British Junior Cup was a brand new initiative for 2015 but whilst it was a slow burner to begin with, by mid-season it was producing some of the most exciting, and certainly the closest, racing on the MCE BSB race programme.

Indeed, more often than not, at least half a dozen riders were contesting the race wins with less than a second between them as they took the chequered flag.

Open to riders aged 13 to 18 years, every rider lined up on an identical 'Cup' variation of the KTM RC 390 with eight events incorporating 20 points scoring races. Former MCE BSB rider Steve Plater was recruited as the Series ambassador, also mentoring the riders along the way.

German youngster Dennis Stelzer had the honour of taking the race wins at the opening round at Donington Park, in his only appearance of the season, but a front pack soon emerged in the shape of Cameron Fraser, Thomas Strudwick, Kevin Keyes and Chris Taylor.

Fraser stole an early march on his rivals before Taylor and 13-year-old Strudwick hit back, the latter particularly impressing as he put together a six-race run at Snetterton, where he became the youngest ever winner of a British Championship race, and then again at Knockhill to lay claim to the title.

However, he then picked up an injury in a non-championship race and missed the next three rounds which allowed Fraser to reassert his control. He was only off the podium just once in the final twelve races and although he only won two of them, it ultimately meant he was crowned champion by a commanding 51 points.

It was Irishman Keyes who eventually took second overall, aided by five wins during the course of the year, whilst Taylor slipped off the pace with three non-scores in the final three races due to a run of bad luck. Like Keyes, he also took five wins during the season.

Strudwick returned at the final round at Silverstone to take his fourth win of the year and clinch fourth overall by just two points from James Nagy whilst Lee Hindle, Aaron Wright and Daniel Drayton all got to stand on the podium at various stages of the season.

The final round of the season, at Silverstone, also saw the World Final take place where just two seconds covered the top 15 in the second race!

CHAMPIONSHIP POSITIONS		
1	Cameron FRASER	337
2	Kevin KEYES	286
3	Chris TAYLOR	271
4	Thomas STRUDWICK	219
5	James NAGY	217
6	Lee HINDLE	182

Ducati TriOptions Cup

ROBBIE SINGS THE TUNE

The Ducati TriOptions Cup was back on the British Superbike Championship programme for a fifth successive year and, like previous seasons, it was again extremely hard fought.

Three riders – Robbie Brown, Leon Morris and Rob Guiver – all arrived at the final round with a chance of taking the win but it was Brown who eventually prevailed.

The former champion had taken a year out of racing in 2014 and it took him a while to get up to speed, but a hat trick of wins at Donington Park in May saw him hit top gear. Five more wins followed, including a crucial one at the final round at Brands Hatch, where a calculated ride saw him take the crown from Morris by 19 points.

Another previous champion, Morris, kept himself in contention with a series of highly consistent finishes which included three wins and nine other podiums, but he could only manage third and fourth at Brands Hatch, as opposed to Brown's first and second, and so had to settle for second overall.

Guiver's challenge was ultimately blunted at the beginning of the season when he only scored points in one of the first four races. That meant he was playing catch up for the rest of the year and although he finished on the podium in all but two of the remaining races, taking three wins along the way, third was where he ended up.

Reigning champion Dennis Hobbs was unable to defend his title in the manner he'd hoped and was never really in the hunt. His season started well with a double victory at the season opener at Brands Hatch but his only other podium finishes came at Knockhill and he was over 100 points adrift of Brown in fourth overall.

Greg Gilfillan and Philip Atkinson both had highly consistent seasons and stood on the podium for the first time, the latter moving up from the Triumph Triple Challenge whilst Darren Fry, Sean Neary and Aaron Brown were also regulars in the leading pack.

Meanwhile, 2013 champion Marty Nutt took five podiums in the first six races and looked set to mount a serious title challenge before announcing his retirement from racing at Knockhill in July.

CHAMPIONSHIP POSITIONS		
1	Robbie BROWN	286
2	Leon MORRIS	267
3	Rob GUIVER	250
4	Dennis HOBBS	175
5	Greg GILFILLAN	159
6	Philip ATKINSON	144

Behind the scenes

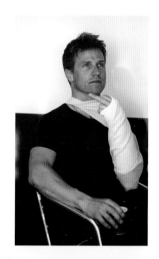

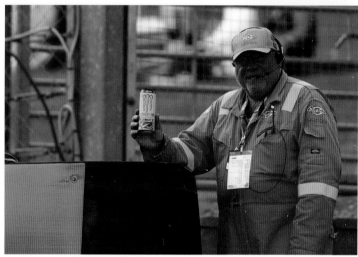

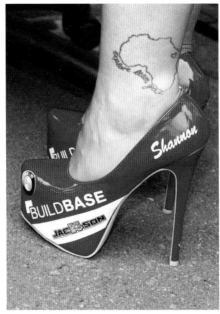

PITLANE
EXIT
CLOSED

MCE British Superbike Championship with Pirelli
Riders points after final round

Name	Total	Gap	Diff	R01 Donington Park 04 April 2015		R02 Brands Hatch Indy 17 April 2015		R03 Oulton Park 04 May 2015		R04 Snetterton 19 June 2015		R05 Knockhill 3 July 2015		R06 Brands Hatch GP 17 July 2015		R07 Thruxton 31 July 2015		R08 Cadwell Park 21 August 2015		R09 Oulton Park 4 September 2015			R10 TT Circuit Assen 18 September 2015		R11 Silverstone 2 October 2015		R12 Brands Hatch GP 16 October 2015			Main Season Wins	Main Season Seconds	Main Season Thirds	Podium Credits
Josh BROOKES (Yamaha)	703			16	10	16	16	20	16	20	20	16	16	25	25	25	25	25	25	13	25	20	25	25	25	25	25	25		7	4	6	53
Shane BYRNE (Kawasaki)	662	41		20	25	20	20	16				25	25	25	25		20	13	20	10	13	25		25	13	11	20	11	20	20	16	7	5	1	51
James ELLISON (Kawasaki)	614	89	48	25	4	25	25	10	20			9			16	13					20	11	11	20	20		11		10	11	20	3	2	1	22
Michael LAVERTY (BMW)	601	102	13	7	9	3				8	13		13	10	11	11	7	10	11		7	9	4	16	7	10	20	7	16	25				
Dan LINFOOT (Honda)	556	147	45	13	20					11	6			4	8			20	11	6	6	11	16	10	2		9	16	3	6	13		2	1	7
Tommy BRIDEWELL (BMW)	545	158	11	10	8				10	25		13	11	9		13		13	16	13	16		16	8		7	9	5	5	4	1	1		2	7
Luke MOSSEY (Kawasaki)	168	535	377	1			4				3	7	3	8		9	9			10	16	9	11	10	13	5		16		6	9	9	10		1	1
Richard COOPER (Kawasaki/BMW)	156	547	12	6		5	1		6	9	6	4		3	20	16			8	9	9	8	9	9	10	4	10						1	1	4
Peter HICKMAN (BMW)	150	553	6	11	13				2	4	1	6	7		3			20	20	6	10		7	3	16	8	4	4	5			2		6
Christian IDDON (Suzuki)	146	557	4	9	11		4		1		7		6	3	8			7	3		7	8	9	10	8	13	13	8	11					
Stuart EASTON (Kawasaki)	139	564	7	5	16	10	11	13	25	9	10	20	20									8	16	20	13	6	4		2	8	7	9	1	2	1	12
Danny BUCHAN (Kawasaki)	125	578	14			2	8			3		10	9									8	16	20	13	6	4		2	8	7	9		1	1	4
Jason O'HALLORAN (Honda)	103	600	22			11	6	9	11	16	16	11	11				7																		2	2
Lee JACKSON (BMW)	101	602	2	3	3			1	6			5	5	4	5		7	4	5	8	5	3	4		5	7	11	10							
Billy McCONNELL (BMW)	98	605	3			7		7	7	2	8		2	4	6	10	8	1	16	10			1	5		3		1						1	1
Howie MAINWARING SMART (Kawasaki)	90	613	8				2	9	9	7	10	8					11	9	1			6			2	5	2	3	6						
John HOPKINS (Ducati)	76	627	14									10											11	5	13		16	13	8					
Chris WALKER (Kawasaki)	67	636	9	8	6	6	3	5	7	10						1		4		1	5	3		8										
James WESTMORELAND (Kawasaki)	66	637	1					3	5			7	8	7	2	16		3	7		6	2										1	1
Ryuichi KIYONARI (BMW)	66	637	0	2		13	13	11							13			2		1	4	7												
Broc PARKES (Yamaha)	38	665	28			8	5					5	5	2	2	5	6																	
Jack KENNEDY (Kawasaki)	35	668	3					1					2	4	9		5	2			3	9												
Martin JESSOPP (BMW)	32	671	3				2					1	6	8		4	4	2			1					1	3							
Jakub SMRZ (Yamaha)	30	673	2																		6	6	3	6	2	7								
Josh WATERS (Suzuki)	28	675	2		1	1		4	4	2			1	2	6		2	1	1	2	1												
Filip BACKLUND (Kawasaki)	19	684	9						8		1	5	2	3																		
Ian HUTCHINSON (Kawasaki)	8	695	11										3	5																		
Adam JENKINSON (Yamaha)	8	695	0										4	3														1				
Luke STAPLEFORD (Kawasaki)	6	697	2																						4			2				
Robbin HARMS (Kawasaki)	4	699	2	4																												
Michael RUTTER (Kawasaki)	3	700	1							3																						
Julien DA COSTA (Honda)	1	702	2																						1							
Jed METCHER (Kawasaki)	1	702	0					1																								

Manufacturers Championship
Points after final round

Name	Total	Gap	Diff	R01		R02		R03		R04		R05		R06		R07		R08		R09			R10		R11		R12		
Kawasaki	541			25	25	25	25	16	25	25	25	25	25	20	20	16	20	10	13	25	20	25	20	20	20	11	20	20	20
Yamaha	531	10		16	10	16	10	16	16	20	16	20	20	16	16	25	25	25	25	25	25	25	25	25	25	25	25	25	7
BMW	377	164	154	11	13	13	13	25	13	13	13	13	13	13	11	8	13	20	20	9	10	16	16	13	16	20	11	16	25
Honda	268	273	109	13	20	11	6	9	11	16	16	11	11	8	7	20	11	6	6	11	16	10	2		9	16	3	6	13
Suzuki	166	375	102	9	11	1	4	4	4	2	7		6	3	8	2	6	7	3	2	7	8	9	10	8	13	13	8	11
Ducati	76	465	90													10							11	5	13		16	13	8

MCE British Superbike Championship with Pirelli
Speedy fastest lap league points after final round

Name	Total	Gap	Diff	R01		R02		R03		R04		R05		R06		R07		R08		R09			R10		R11		R12		
Josh BROOKES (Yamaha)	16							2								2		1	1	2	2	2	1				1	1	
Shane BYRNE (Kawasaki)	13	3		2	1			2	1	1		2	1							1					2			1	1
James ELLISON (Kawasaki)	7	9	6			2	2					1				2									2			
Dan LINFOOT (Honda)	1	15	6													1												
Howie MAINWARING SMART (Kawasaki)	1	15	0																								1	

Motorpoint British Supersport Championship

Riders points after final round

Round dates: R01 Donington Park 04 April 2015 · R02 Brands Hatch Indy 17 April 2015 · R03 Oulton Park 04 May 2015 · R04 Snetterton 19 June 2015 · R05 Knockhill 3 July 2015 · R06 Brands Hatch GP 17 July 2015 · R07 Thruxton 31 July 2015 · R08 Cadwell Park 21 August 2015 · R09 Oulton Park 4 September 2015 · R10 TT Circuit Assen 18 September 2015 · R11 Silverstone 2 October 2015 · R12 Brands Hatch GP 16 October 2015

Name	Total	Gap	Diff	R1a	R1b	R2a	R2b	R3a	R3b	R4a	R4b	R5a	R5b	R6a	R6b	R7a	R7b	R8a	R8b	R9a	R9b	R10a	R10b	R11a	R11b	R12a	R12b
Luke STAPLEFORD	471			25	20	16	25	25		25		20	13	25	25	25	25	25	20	16	16	25	25	25		25	25
Kyle RYDE	344	127		13	16	25	20	16	20	20		16	25	20	20	20	10	20	16			10	11	11	11	11	13
Jake DIXON	337	134	7	20	25	13	16		25		11		20		10	6	16	16	25	20	25	16	20	13		20	20
Glenn IRWIN	320	151	17	16	13	20	13	20	13	11	25	25	16		8	10	13	11	9		13	11	16	16	25		16
James RISPOLI	256	215	64		9		11			13	20	11	10	13	13	16		13	13	11	20	20				13	10
Ben WILSON	185	286	71	10	10	10	10		10					9	7	8	9	9	11	10	11	9	10	9	13	9	11
Sam HORNSEY	181	290	4	5		11			9			13	11	11	11	13	8			13		13	13	16		16	
Luke HEDGER	168	303	13					10		10	16	10	8	10	9	9	11	8	10	8	10		7	7	10	7	8
Andy REID	165	306	3	11	11					13	16	16				16	16	11	20	10		25					
Joe COLLIER	147	324	18	9	7	6	6	11	11	7	10	7	9	7	6	2	5	4		6	7		2	6	5	8	6
Danny WEBB	135	336	12		6	9	9	8	7	9	13	9	4			7	7		4	7		8	9		9	3	7
Marshall NEILL	97	374	38	7	5	4		2	5	8		5	7			3	5	2	3	5	5	5	5	6	6	4	
Dean HIPWELL	87	384	10	8		8		9	8	6		3	3	8	5		6		2		9	4	5	2	1		
Matthew PAULO	64	407	23					1	2	4	6	8	6		2		1	7	7	4	6		3	3	2	2	
Jamie PERRIN	64	407	0	6		5	3	6		2	8			5		3	4					4	7	6	5		
Bjorn ESTMENT	61	410	3	2	3	7	8		3			4		6		4	3	6		3	3					5	4
Joe FRANCIS	50	421	11																	7	8	8	8	10	9
Harry HARTLEY	46	425	4				8		7	7						5	6			9			4				
Sam COVENTRY	43	428	3	3		3	4	5			4	2		3	4			2		2	4				3	1	3
Levi DAY	42	429	1	4	4	1				3	4	5	9	6	5	1											
Freddy PETT	21	450	21				1					3	3			4	1		1			2		1	4		1
Luke JONES	15	456	6	1				2	5				7														
Keith FARMER	13	458	2																1		3	1	8				
Josh DAY	13	458	0				2				1	4	6														
Niall CAMPBELL	10	461	3						2				2		2	2					2						
Ben STAFFORD	6	465	4																			6					
Josh DALEY	6	465	0										5								1						
David ALLINGHAM	4	467	2														1						3				
Phil WAKEFIELD	3	468	1								1	1	1														
Sam THOMPSON	2	469	1																								2
Tommy PHILP	2	469	0																		1	1					
Matt TRUELOVE	1	470	1																						1		
Paul CURRAN	1	470	0									1															

Motorpoint British Supersport Championship

Top 15 riders - EVO points after final round

Name	Total	Gap	Diff	R1a	R1b	R2a	R2b	R3a	R3b	R4a	R4b	R5a	R5b	R6a	R6b	R7a	R7b	R8a	R8b	R9a	R9b	R10a	R10b	R11a	R11b	R12a	R12b
Joe COLLIER	500			25	25	20	20	25	25	20	25	20	25	25	25	13	25	16		25	25	9	16	25	16	25	25
Marshall NEILL	358	142		20	20	13		10	16	25		13	20		16	25	13	13	20	20	16	20	25	20	20	13	
Matthew PAULO	264	236	94					9	10	13	11	25	16	8	13	8	11	16	25	16	25	20		13	10	11	
Bjorn ESTMENT	237	263	27	10	13	25	25				11			11		20		20	16	20		13	11		10	16	16
Jamie PERRIN	229	271	8	16				16	11	20		10	16			16		16	20	11			7	16	25	20	20
Sam COVENTRY	214	286	15	11		11	8	11	13	16		7	9	10		11	20	9		11	13	10	10	11	10	13	
Freddy PETT	184	316	30				10	6	7	6	6	11	8			13	11	11		10	11	8	6	13	7	11	13
Niall CAMPBELL	149	351	35	7	6				10	4		6	7		11	10	9	10		6	10	7	10	4	8	7	7
Levi DAY	144	356	5	13	16	9	8	11	13	16	20	16	13	9													
Josh DALEY	133	367	11	3	3	7	6	8	3	8	10					7	7	7	9	9	16	10	4			9	7
David ALLINGHAM	124	376	9								4	8	10			5	10	5	10	9		9		16	11	9	9
Phil WAKEFIELD	109	391	15	6	7			5		5	9	9	6	7		1	5	4	8	8	13	6	8	2			
Ryan DIXON	75	425	34	1	4				1	3	7	5				6	8	3	8	4	6	5	8	2	5		3
Tommy PHILP	72	428	3													4	6	6			7	5	7	11	1	8	8
Josh DAY	61	439	11				11	8	9	13	20																

Motorpoint British Supersport Championship

Speedy fastest lap league points after final round

Name	Total	Gap	Diff	R1a	R1b	R2a	R2b	R3a	R3b	R4a	R4b	R5a	R5b	R6a	R6b	R7a	R7b	R8a	R8b	R9a	R9b	R10a	R10b	R11a	R11b	R12a	R12b
Luke STAPLEFORD	20										1		2	1		2	1			1		2		2	1	2		1	2
Jake DIXON	8	12				1	1						2	2					2									
Kyle RYDE	4	16	4					2	2																		
James RISPOLI	3	17	1															2							1		
Andy REID	2	18	1								1											1					

Pirelli National Superstock 1000 Championship with Black Horse
Riders points after final round

Name	Total	Gap	Diff	Donington Park 04 April 2015	Brands Hatch Indy 17 April 2015	Oulton Park 02 May 2015	Donington Park WSBK 23 May 2015	Snetterton 19 June 2015	Knockhill 3 July 2015	Brands Hatch GP 17 July 2015	Thruxton 31 July 2015	Cadwell Park 21 August 2015	Oulton Park 4 September 2015	Silverstone 3 October 2015	Brands Hatch GP 18 October 2015
Joshua ELLIOTT	245			20	25	20	20	25	25		20	25	20	20	25
Alastair SEELEY	193	52		16	11	25	16	20		25	25	20	25	10	
Husdon KENNAUGH	166	79	27	25	16	16	25	16			11	16	16	25	
Luke QUIGLEY	127	118	39	10	9	13	11	13		13	3	13	13	16	13
Adam JENKINSON	104	141	23	13	20	10					13	10	9	13	16
James EAST	100	145	4	3	7	8	8	6		16	10	11	11		20
Jesse TRAYLER	94	151	6	6	10	7		11	13	20	8			8	11
Michael ROBERTSON	64	181	30	9			10	9	20	9		5		2
Josh WAINWRIGHT	54	191	10		3		6			7	7	9	7	9	6
Dominic USHER	54	191	0	7	1	9		7			5	8	8		9
Alex OLSEN	53	192	1		8	1		4	11	11	16	2			
James EGAN	45	200	8	5		2	7	8	8	10		5			
Ashley BEECH	40	205	5	11				10			4	7			8
Tom TUNSTALL	39	206	1					1	10	8	1	3	6	5	5
Joe BURNS	30	215	9								9		10	11	
John INGRAM	26	219	4			5		5	16						
Ben GODFREY	25	220	1				9				2		4	7	3
Johnny BLACKSHAW	25	220	0			4	4			4				6	7
Nick ANDERSON	21	224	4				3	3	5	6		4			
Leon JEACOCK	19	226	2			6			7		6				
Mike BOOTH	15	230	4		2		2		4				2	1	4
Barry TEASDALE	14	231	1		5				9						
Tom FISHER	14	231	0					2		5		1	3	3	
Richard COOPER	13	232	1				13								
James ROSE	13	232	0		13										
David JOHNSON	11	234	2			11									
Keith FARMER	10	235	1												10
Nico MAWHINNEY	10	235	0	4				5						1	
Dan KNEEN	8	237	2	8											
Kyle WILKS	8	237	0	2	4		1			1					
Rob McNEALY	8	237	0			3				2	2				1
Billy MELLOR	6	239	2									6			
Johnathan RAILTON	6	239	0						6						
Josh CORNER	6	239	0		6										
Sam WEST	6	239	0						1	3			2		
Fraser ROGERS	4	241	2										4		
Daniel HEGARTY	3	242	1						3						
Alex HEATON	1	244	2	1											

Pirelli National Superstock 600 Championship with Black Horse
Riders points after final round

Name	Total	Gap	Diff	Donington Park 04 April 2015	Brands Hatch Indy 17 April 2015	Oulton Park 02 May 2015	Donington Park WSBK 23 May 2015	Snetterton 19 June 2015	Knockhill 3 July 2015	Brands Hatch GP 17 July 2015	Thruxton 31 July 2015	Cadwell Park 21 August 2015	Oulton Park 4 September 2015	Silverstone 3 October 2015	Brands Hatch GP 18 October 2015
Mason LAW	239			25	25	25	25		16	13	25	25	20	20	20
Benjamin CURRIE	180	59		20	20	2	20	25	13	20	11		11	25	13
Tarran MACKENZIE	177	62	3	8	16			13	20	25	25	20		25		25
Andrew IRWIN	103	136	74	1	10			13	20	16	3	13		11	16
Joe FRANCIS	103	136	0	16	9	16		16	11	9	13		13		
Jordan WEAVING	78	161	25				4	11	8		8	20	16		11
Bradley JONES	71	168	7	13	8	11			1	3	1	16	5	10	3
Ross TWYMAN	67	172	4	10		7		3			7	9	9	13	9
Chrissy ROUSE	67	172	0		11	9		9	10	7	6			8	7
Dan STAMPER	61	178	6		5	8	16	10	4	8	10				
Tom WARD	56	183	5		2			7	8			6	7	16	10
Malachi MITCHELL THOMAS	56	183	0	11	6	13		6	9	11					
Bradley RAY	53	186	3			20			6	10	9				8
Ben STAFFORD	48	191	5	7		4	10	4	3	2		10	8		
George STANLEY	39	200	9	4		5	11				5	1	1	6	6
Matt TRUELOVE	36	203	3		13			1				7	6	9	
Wayne RYAN	32	207	4						5	6	16				5
Kevin VAN LEUVEN	32	207	0	9	3	3	8		2				2	5	
Tom CARNE	27	212	5	5		10	5	2		5					
Keenan ARMSTRONG	23	216	4						4	4	8		7		
Daniel MURPHY	22	217	1				1				11	10			
Tom OLIVER	20	219	2	6		6					4		4		
Carl PHILLIPS	14	225	6				3	7			2				2
Tom BOOTH AMOS	10	229	4				9						1		
James EDWARDS	10	229	0	3	7										
Jordan GILBERT	10	229	0			1	2						3		4
Lewis ROLLO	7	232	3							7					
Harry TRUELOVE	7	232	0								5		2	
Ben LUXTON	6	233	1				6								
Fraser ROGERS	6	233	0					5		1					
Sam THOMPSON	6	233	0	2	4										
Dale THOMAS	4	235	2									4		
Matthew WIGLEY	3	236	1										3	
Davey TODD	3	236	0								3			
Tom NEAVE	2	237	1								2			
Liam SHELLCOCK	1	238	1											1
Ashley BUXTON	1	238	0		1									

HEL Performance British Motostar Championship - 125GP

Riders points after final round

Name	Total	Gap	Diff	Donington Park 04 April 2015		Brands Hatch Indy 17 April 2015		Oulton Park 02 May 2015		Snetterton 19 June 2015		Knockhill 3 July 2015		Brands Hatch GP 17 July 2015		Thruxton 31 July 2015		Cadwell Park 21 August 2015		Oulton Park 4 September 2015		TT Circuit Assen 18 September 2015		Silverstone 2 October 2015		Brands Hatch GP 16 October 2015	
Josh OWENS	435			10	25	25	25	25	25	25	25	25	20	25	20	25		20	25	13			20	25	25	16	16
Mark CLAYTON	270	165		16	10	16	13	20	10	20	13	13	13	13	13	16		13	16	11		20	13		8	8	8
Andrew SAWFORD	255	180	15	25	20	20				16	13	13	20		9	11		20	9			16	20	10	13		9	11
Liam DELVES	249	186	6	11	13	7	8	10	7	9		16	16	7	8	8	20	9	10	16		16	9	16	16	11	6
Wesley JONKER	246	189	3	13	16	9	10	11	20	16				8	9			13	9	20		16	20	20	13	13
Cameron HORSMAN	228	207	18	6	7		9				11		25	20	25		25	25			25	25	25				
Tasia RODINK	183	252	45	8	8	11	7	5		9	8	10	9	10	10	10	11	11	7	8			11	13	10	7	
Stephen CAMPBELL	179	256	4	9		8	11	7			6	11	10	11			13	10			13	11	10	9	11	10	10
Jamie EDWARDS	176	259	3	4	11	13	16	9		11	10	8	8		9	11	16		11	7				10	9	6	7
Jamie ASHBY	141	294	35	7	6	5	6	6		6	8	7		9	7	6	7	7	8	6	9			8	5	5	3
Ryan LONGSHAW	131	304	10	20	9	10	20	13		16				11		16	16										
Louis VALLELEY	63	372	68		5	6		8								6		5	10	8		6			9
Taz TAYLOR	50	385	13																						25	25
David WALES	46	389	4					5	5			5	6			5	5					6	4	3	2
Bradley RAY	40	395	6																					20	20
Roman RAJEK	29	406	11																			11	13		5
Clint CLARKE	22	413	7																	7		7		4	4
Adam MOORE	14	421	8		3			5		6															
Edgar MACHADO	13	422	1													7	6							
Steve LAWTON	8	427	5															8						
Sam LLEWELLYN	7	428	1																			7		
Alex WOOD	5	430	2																		5			
Bryn OWEN	5	430	0	5																				

HEL Performance British Motostar Championship - MOTO 3

Riders points after final round

Name	Total	Gap	Diff	Donington Park 04 April 2015		Brands Hatch Indy 17 April 2015		Oulton Park 02 May 2015		Snetterton 19 June 2015		Knockhill 3 July 2015		Brands Hatch GP 17 July 2015		Thruxton 31 July 2015		Cadwell Park 21 August 2015		Oulton Park 4 September 2015		TT Circuit Assen 18 September 2015		Silverstone 2 October 2015		Brands Hatch GP 16 October 2015	
Scott DEROUE	473				25	20	25	13		25	20	20	20	20	25	20	25	20	25	25		20	25	25	25	25	25
Taz TAYLOR	354	119		20	16	25	20	25			25	25	25	25	20	25	13	25		25				20	20		
Edward RENDELL	262	211	92	16	13	16	16	20		16	16	13	16	8	16		11			10	7	20		16	16	16	
Dani SAEZ	228	245	34		11	8	9	8	20		16	10	13	13	16	16			11		13	16	11		20	20
Jorel BOERBOOM	222	251	6		10	10	13	10			13		13	11	11	6	8	11	20	11	10	16	11	13	9	16
Charlie NESBITT	174	299	48	13			8	13			7	10	11	11	8	16		13	20	16	6				6	13
Jake ARCHER	162	311	12				3	7	6	11			1			9		11	10	13	13	20	11	13	13	10	11
Vasco VAN DER VALK	158	315	4	9	4	1	2	1		4	7	8	9	7	7	5	4	10	11	9	8	10	10	11	10	11
Elliot LODGE	143	330	15	8	6	5	5	6		9		10	7	6	9	4	3	7	9	5	2	6	9	9	8	10
Georgina POLDEN	121	352	22	13			8	9		8		2	6	4	8	10	6	5	8	7	1	8	6	6		6
Mike BROUWERS	119	354	2	3			1			6	3	4		5	10	8	7	8	10	8	9	9	8	7	13
Alex PERSSON	106	367	13			9	11	16		13	9	9	11	10		9	9								
Brian SLOOTEN	105	368	1	7	7	4	7	3		5	6			3	5	2		6	5	6	5	5	7	8	5	9
Joe THOMAS	67	406	38	11	9	2	4	2	2	2		6		2	6	3	2		3		2	3	1	4
Christoph BEINLICH	52	421	15			11	10	4		11	10			7		5				3		3	5	3	
Richard KERR	51	422	1	4								7	5	1	3	3	16	3		3	5		3
Edmund BEST	49	424	2		2				4	1	3	1		7	5	9	6			5	2	2	2
Brad RAY	45	428	4	25	20																				
Tomas DE VRIES	43	430	2	5	1			3	1	3	2			4						4	4		5
Joseph THOMPSON	30	443	13	10	5	3		7	5													
Joel MARKLUND	26	447	4	6		6		5		5	4										
Ernst DUBBINK	20	453	6														13	7			
Chris TAYLOR	15	458	5																	7	8
Ryan LONGSHAW	12	461	3																1		4	7
TJ TOMS	11	462	1					1				3	2	4			1		
Sam BURMAN	10	463	1									2	1	2	4				1
Dennis KOOPMAN	6	467	4											4	2		
Walid SOPPE	4	469	2												4		
Asher DURHAM	3	470	1					3									
Sven GREVINK	1	472	2												1		

Santander Consumer Finance KTM British Junior Cup
Riders points after final round

Name	Total	Gap	Diff	Donington Park 04 April 2015		Brands Hatch Indy 17 April 2015			Snetterton 19 June 2015		Knockhill 3 July 2015				Thruxton 31 July 2015			Cadwell Park 21 August 2015		Oulton Park 4 September 2015		Silverstone 2 October 2015	
Cameron FRASER	337			11		25	25	20	16		13	16	16	16	20	25	16	25	20	20	20	13	20
Kevin KEYES	286	51				20	11	25	13	13	9	20	25	11	25	20	20	11		13	25	25	
Chris TAYLOR	271	66	15		16	16	20	16	25	20	25	9			20			9	25	20	25	25	
Thomas STRUDWICK	219	118	52	20	10	13	16				20	25	20	25	20	25						25	
James NAGY	217	120	2		20	11	13	13	16		16	13	13	13	13	13		13	16	16	11	20	13
Lee HINDLE	182	155	35	16	9	10	9	10	11	11	6	10	11		10	11		10	11	10		11	16
Reece GUYETT	166	171	16	11	7	8	7	7	10	10	10	7		10	8	7	9	9	9	8	9	10	10
Aaron WRIGHT	161	176	5	10	6	9	5	11		9	8	8	9	9	16	10		7	6	9	13	16	
Daniel DRAYTON	125	212	36								11	11	10		11	13	13	16	13	11	16		
Oliver O'FLAHERTY	102	235	23	9	5	4	3	5	6	8	9	7			6	3	8	8		6	7	8	
Sam LYONS	102	235	0	8	4	4	3	5	7	5	3	5	7	4	9	6	11			6	7	8	
Thomas AIREY	90	247	12						5	3	5	2	4	5	6	5	8	5	7	5	10	9	11
Ewan POTTER	69	268	21	6	2	2	2	3	4	2	2		2	2	7	4	7	4	5	3	5	7	
Myles WASLEY	68	269	1	13	8	5	8	9	8	4	1	6	6										
James HOBSON	60	277	8	13		7	10		8		7	4	8	3									
Dennis STELZER	50	287	10	25	25																		
Kieran STYLES	38	299	12	7	3	3	1	4												2	4	8	6
Gary WINFIELD	23	314	15															8		7	8		
Lewis PATERSON	19	318	4								4	3	5	7									
Josh OWENS	16	321	3												16								
Adam PHIPPS	15	322	1																	6		9	
Danny BOJ	14	323	1															6	8				
Harrison DAY	12	325	2						6	6													
Kai MASTERS	10	327	2																	10			
Jack WARING	10	327	0				4	6															
Ben MASTERS	4	333	6																	4			

Ducati TriOptions Cup
Riders points after final round

Name	Total	Gap	Diff	Brands Hatch Indy 17 April 2015 (1)	(2)	Oulton Park 02 May 2015 (1)	(2)	Donington Park WSBK 23 May 2015 (1)	(2)	Knockhill 03 July 2015 (1)	(2)	Cadwell Park 21 August 2015 (1)	(2)	TT Circuit Assen 18 September 2015	Silverstone 02 October 2015 (1)	(2)	Brands Hatch GP 16 October 2015 (1)	(2)
Robbie BROWN	286			11	8	16	25	25	25		11	25	25	25	20	25	20	25
Leon MORRIS	267	19		16	10	25	20	16	13	25	16	20	16	20	25	16	16	13
Rob GUIVER	250	36	17			20	20	16	13	25	20	25	20	10	16	20	25	20
Dennis HOBBS	175	111	75	25	25			13	10	20	20	13	11	9	9	11	9	
Greg GILFILLAN	159	127	16	7	11	5	10	9	9	16	13	10	10	11	16	13	10	9
Philip ATKINSON	144	142	15	6		9	6	8	8	7	16	16	13	11	10	13	11	10
Darren FRY	139	147	5	10	9	10	11	11	11	9	7	9	10	6	9	11	8	8
Sean NEARY	136	150	3	13	13			7	7	10	11	13	7	13	8	10	13	11
Aaron BROWN	128	158	8	8	7	9	13	10	7	10	9	8	8	6	8		9	16
Marty NUTT	105	181	23	20	16	20		16	13	20								
Mark CHEETHAM	73	213	32			2	11	8	3	2	8	8	5	5	3	6	7	5
Louis DAWSON	57	229	16	5				6	5	5		6		6	7	4	7	6
David FERNS	41	245	16				4	6	2	4	5	6	5	6	2	1		
Jody LEES	36	250	5	4	4	7		7	8	6								
William MONIE	35	251	1						3	11	8	3	7		3			
James SHAW	33	253	2	2	1		8	3	4	5						7	2	1
Sean GILFILLAN	31	255	2				3	4				6	9		4	3	2	
Craig CURRY	28	258	3	9	6							4	3	2		4		
Jon WAGHORN	28	258	0	3	5				1	1	1			5	2		4	6
Danny HILL	21	265	7						2	3	5	5			1			5
Taryn SKINNER	15	271	6						1			4				2	1	7
Nicky WILSON	15	271	0	1					2	1	4	1	4					2
Carl STEVENS	14	272	1									1	2	4	3			4
Ross HUMPHRIES	12	274	2							2	2	3			5			
Alistair FAGAN	6	280	6											1	3	1	1	
Mike HONEY	3	283	3															3
Ben BROADWAY	3	283	0			3												

seeing**red** ₂₀₁₅